ZAK GEORGE'S
DOG TRAINING REVOLUTION

ZAK GEORGE'S
DOG TRAINING REVOLUTION

The Complete Guide to Raising the Perfect Pet with Love

Zak George
with Dina Roth Port

TEN SPEED PRESS
Berkeley

To all the people who have supported
the Dog Training Revolution and helped raise
the standards for how we teach dogs.
This revolution exists because of you. Thank you.

CONTENTS

ACKNOWLEDGMENTS

My coauthor, Dina, and I have many people to thank. First, our enormous gratitude to our literary agent, Al Zuckerman, for championing this book from day one. Your guidance, knowledge, and unwavering support are invaluable to us. We also thank our editor, Lisa Westmoreland, for your enthusiasm and dedication to our book. Much gratitude to you, Kara Plikaitis, and the rest of the team at Ten Speed Press for your hard work.

We thank Dr. Rudd Nelson, Dr. Bruce Tannenbaum, and Dr. Meghan Herron for graciously offering your expertise. Also, a huge thanks to Leslie Nelson for helping with this book every step of the way and to Lisa Pansini for sharing your creativity and vision.

From Zak

I want to thank my dad for his unwavering, lifelong support both personally and professionally. He is one of the most positive, loving people I've ever known, and I wouldn't have been able to accomplish as much as I have without him. My mom deserves a tremendous amount of recognition for always encouraging me to do my best. Her drive and determination to make the world a better place are contagious. I love you both very much.

My girlfriend, Bree, the love of my life, has been one of my biggest inspirations and so supportive over the last several years. I look forward to a bright future with you, Brianna. The Dog Training Revolution wouldn't be the same without you.

My dogs, Venus, Supernova, and Alpha Centauri, have taught me much more than I could ever teach them. I especially want to acknowledge Venus. Some people are fortunate to meet that once-in-a-lifetime dog; however, you rarely meet one who completely changes the trajectory of your life. For me, that dog is Venus. She truly is my superstar.

For years I've wanted to do this book, but I knew that it would be too huge of an undertaking. Thank you, Dina, my coauthor, for being so determined and for sharing the same vision to enlighten everyday dog lovers to understand their dogs more deeply than ever before. If it weren't for you, this book would not exist. I will be eternally grateful for your dedication to the Dog Training Revolution.

From Dina

I would like to thank my parents for your constant support and love. Thank you for nurturing my love for animals so many years ago.

I could never adequately express my deep appreciation for my husband, Larry. You are always there for me, ready to read over a chapter, help in a pinch when I'm on deadline, and provide technical assistance or words of encouragement. Your strength, wisdom, and sense of humor can help me get through anything. I love you very much.

Thank you to our children, Samantha and Zachary, who make me proud every day. You always know just how to put a smile on my face. You are also both so supportive of my work, and that means the world to me. I hope you know that *you* are my greatest accomplishments. I admire and adore you both.

Zak, it has been such fun and a true pleasure to write this book with you. You are so passionate about helping guide the dog training industry toward methods that are not only the most effective but also ethical, kind, and science-based. I am honored to help you spread your important message. You are making the world a better place for these beloved animals. Thank you for everything.

Lastly, I want to thank my muses, Baxter and Brody, who sat by my feet as I cowrote this book. You provide my family with affection, friendship, unconditional love, and plenty of laughs. The two of you, along with Champ and Barkley, have enriched my life more than you'll ever know. (Yes, you too, Kitty Cupcake.)

INTRODUCTION

Few things in this world are more exciting and more memorable than welcoming a new dog into your life. The journey goes far beyond simply having a companion by your side. Dogs have much to teach us: They always live in the moment. They're never spiteful, and they don't hold grudges. Also, there's just something about dogs' loyalty and unconditional love that makes people crazy about them.

That's not to say that bringing a dog home doesn't come with its challenges. You have a lot to teach your new pet so that you can live in harmony and have a long, rewarding relationship. Whether you are reading this book because you've just gotten a dog or because you want some fresh perspective on raising the one you already have, I promise you that you have come to the right place.

Like many people, I have always adored dogs. I grew up with an adorable terrier mix named Raisin, and I learned that dogs are independent-minded beings who have a great capacity for love.

As I got older, my love for dogs continued to grow. I was absolutely fascinated by them—I'd watch dog Frisbee competitions on TV and was blown away by their flips, leaps, and other tricks. I just couldn't wrap my head around the idea that a dog and a person could communicate so well, and I really wanted to experience that. So in my twenties, I decided it was time to raise a dog on my own. Little did I know that my life was about to take a turn from average to amazing: that's when I got Venus.

Venus is a Border Collie, and from the minute I met her I was so impressed by her intelligence. I spent a lot of time training her and always made it fun. In turn, we became completely in tune with each other, and she seemed as obsessed with learning as I was with teaching. I found that there was virtually no limit to what she could do. In just a few days, she learned how to fake a limp by walking on three legs—total Hollywood style, really convincing. Then there's my favorite trick I call "Superstar"—I'd lie on my back and Venus would balance on her hind legs on *top* of the soles of my feet. Next, I'd throw Frisbees to her, one after the other. She'd catch every one while maintaining her balance! However, while I know part of her success was due to the amount of time I dedicated to her, it was our bond that played an even bigger role. Venus showed me that *when you prioritize your relationship with your dog, the teaching process becomes easy.*

When Venus was about ten months old, I decided to drop my real estate career and figure out how I could somehow make a living while teaching her. Of course this job didn't exist, but I found something surprisingly close. By this point, Venus had won her first three Frisbee competitions, and I found out that a PetSmart near my house was looking for a dog trainer. I scheduled an interview and brought Venus and our three trophies as my resumé. Venus and I performed for the interviewer. I was hired on the spot.

I enjoyed my time at PetSmart over the next few years—it gave me tons of experience. After that, I continued training and, in total, taught thousands of dogs and their families. I worked with all different breeds and mixed breeds and handled virtually every behavioral issue you can imagine. I also added two more Border Collies to my family—Alpha Centauri and Supernova—and eventually took a job with Stunt Dog Productions, performing with my three dogs nationwide. In 2006, I also launched my YouTube channel, now known as *Zak George's Dog Training Revolution*, posting videos on how to teach dogs everything from "roll over" to how to stop them from jumping up. I quickly acquired more subscribers than any other dog trainer on YouTube, a status that holds today. Eventually, my success led to my starring on my first TV show, Animal Planet's *SuperFetch*, on which I taught average people how to teach their dogs awesome tricks. Later, I produced and starred on a BBC show called *Who Let the Dogs Out?*, a talent search for Britain's best young dog trainers.

Throughout all of this experience, I showed people that by learning to connect with their dogs and have fun with them, they could teach them extraordinary things. However, I was also shocked by the scary amount of misinformation in the dog training world. I heard a lot of talk about how we have to be our dogs' pack leaders and that we need to dominate them; otherwise they will attempt to be the "alpha." I saw very well-known traditional trainers tell people that dogs are essentially wolves at heart and should be treated as such, even though the actual science tells a very different story. Dogs did descend from ancient wolves, *but this next point is critical*: for thousands of years, humans have specifically bred dogs for different skills, such as herding, retrieving, or simply for companionship. In other words, dogs have been bred to interact with people. Catering to the wolf ancestry rather than acknowledging this selective breeding ignores why the modern dog even exists, and any training method that teaches based on this old-fashioned line of thinking is fundamentally flawed.

Unfortunately, traditional dog training, which relies heavily on dominance theory, often means punishment-based training. People are told to use force and intimidation to teach their dogs to be submissive. This has always bothered me, not just because it can be very unpleasant for the dog, but also because it focuses on *making* dogs act a certain way rather than encouraging them to *want* to do so. For instance, tools designed to cause discomfort to dogs in the name of teaching are commonplace today. I know that many of you reading this may have purchased these devices—such as metal collars, choke chains, and prong collars—in the past, but I also understand that you likely bought them under the advisement of an expert you trusted. I will offer you a better option—one that will teach your dog faster without the use of these tools or other harsh corrections, which do nothing to promote a bond between a person and a dog.

My mission has become clear: to give people an alternative to the shallow, older ways of training dogs. I, along with other like-minded dog professionals, have set out to help raise the standards in dog training and show people that only through heartfelt communication, not domination, can they expect incredible results. And I've been overwhelmed by the response: today, over a decade into my career, I see more people embracing positive training methods than ever before. Meanwhile, the American Veterinary Society of Animal Behavior, the Association of Professional Dog Trainers, and countless professionals have come out against dominance theory, saying that it hinders training, harms relationships between humans and dogs, and actually can *cause* behavioral problems.[1] I am proud that we all have helped to disrupt an industry headed down the wrong path. Together, we have truly been part of a Dog Training Revolution.

Now this book will help you become a part of it, as it will teach you not only the most humane training techniques but also the most effective. It also takes into account that all dogs are different and will show you how to teach *your* dog. I'll help you every step of the way. I'll walk you through everything you need to know—from picking out your dog and housetraining to feeding, basic training, socialization, grooming, and health issues. This book includes a shopping list, a guide to dog-proofing your home, what to do in case of an emergency, and other checklists. I'll also help troubleshoot common behavioral problems, such as excessive barking, chewing, nipping, and jumping, and even offer advice on the extra fun stuff, such as traveling, exercising with your dog, and cool tricks. And most important, every bit of advice I give works toward building such a strong bond between you and your dog that you'll be astounded by what you can train her to do. After all, the person who can best train your dog is the person who knows her best—and that's you. My job is simply to show you how.

Think of this book as your trusty go-to guide. Keep it somewhere handy. Read it straight through or take a chapter at a time. Afterward, you can search the index for topics you need help with as they arise.

 **LOOK OUT FOR THIS SYMBOL**

Use my YouTube videos as vivid illustrations along the way—look out for the play-button icon that will let you know which topics have corresponding companion videos. Then head over to my website at www.dogtrainingrevolution.com, where I'll link to those videos in order by chapter.

You're doing a wonderful thing by welcoming a dog into your home. Now get ready to learn what you can do to set the stage for what can be one of the most loving, fulfilling relationships you'll ever have.

CHAPTER ONE

DECISIONS, DECISIONS: CHOOSING THE RIGHT DOG FOR YOU

Sure, there are plenty of people who wander into a pet store or shelter, fall madly in love with an adorable puppy, and bring him home that day. However, it's always important to remember that choosing a dog is a huge commitment, one that can last for fifteen years or more. It's crucial to do your homework.

Far too many people decide to get a dog on a whim, and they wind up having to give their pet away after they realize they just can't handle the responsibility. Sadly, these precious animals often wind up in animal shelters where, according to the American Society for the Prevention of Cruelty to Animals (ASPCA), 1.2 million dogs are euthanized each year.[1] Many others wind up living months or years in cages, waiting for someone to adopt them.

We can avoid this, and the key is knowing what to expect *before* you get a dog. While bringing one into your family can be one of life's most joyous experiences, it also requires a lot of time, patience, consistency, and love. Puppies or older dogs who have not had significant training require several weeks just for you to start establishing basic communication with them. After that come months of training. If you are considering getting a dog, this chapter will help you determine whether that's the best decision for you right now. Then, if it is, it's a matter of finding the *right* dog for your lifestyle so that you can meet your pet's needs and help him fit seamlessly into your family. Let's get started!

THE MOST IMPORTANT CONSIDERATIONS

When thinking about getting a dog, remember they *all* need the following things.

Time

Dogs are highly intelligent, social creatures who require mental and physical stimulation every day. Moderate- to high-energy dogs need considerable exercise, such as a long run or an extended game of fetch. Caring for a new dog and training him requires a lot of time; you can't cut corners and expect the results you want. So if you work eighty hours a week and are never home, don't get a dog unless either you have a trusted relative or friend who will care for your pet or you're prepared to hire a dog walker on a regular basis. Also, if you like to be out and about all weekend and don't want the "hassle" of having to come home throughout the day to walk a dog, you might want to reconsider getting one.

Prepare to spend twenty minutes to one hour a day of training and exercise at least five days a week for the first six months to a year. Don't worry, it doesn't take that long to teach the fundamentals; we can do that in less than two months. However, if you dedicate that extra time to training, then you can expect spectacular results. Our dogs can be with us for a long time, so why not put in extra time up front so you'll have an incredibly well-behaved dog for years to come?

Patience

It's important to set your expectations: Your new dog *will* make mistakes and do things you're not happy about. He may play bite for months, and potty accidents in the house are almost inevitable. Dogs can be noisy and messy, and they certainly won't pick up the toys they leave around the house. If you're getting a dog, you've got to be willing to get into the mindset that this is all normal and remember there's a light at the end of the tunnel. Make the commitment right now to prioritize patience. The irony about teaching dogs is that the faster you try to get results, the slower your progress will be. Take your time and you'll achieve success sooner.

Costs

People often underestimate the costs of taking care of a dog. There's the initial expense—which can range from a minimal donation at a shelter to $2,000 or more for a puppy that comes from a pet store or breeder. However, the costs don't end there and will vary greatly depending on the size and age of your dog, his grooming needs, where you live, and personal choice.

At first, there are the basic supplies, ranging from a collar and leash to a crate and food, a veterinarian checkup, and possibly neutering or spaying. You'll have annual expenses such as food, vet visits and medications, toys, and supplies. Bills can also skyrocket for those people who hire professional dog walkers or groomers on a regular basis, dog sitters for when they travel, or trainers. Lastly, there are those unexpected expenses—say, when your dog eats a pair of underwear and has to have it surgically removed (a reason to consider pet health insurance; see page 39, chapter 2). Bottom line: Whether you pay a hefty sum for a dog or get one for free from a friend, the cost of caring for one can range from about $1,000 a year to ten times that.

LIFESTYLE ISSUES

Once you've determined whether you have the time, patience, and financial means to care for a dog, think about the following questions.

Where Do You Live?

Many apartments buildings don't allow dogs; other communities restrict certain breeds or set weight limits for dogs. Make sure you ask your landlord or homeowners' association which rules apply to you. Also, look at your environment and determine whether your dog's exercise needs can be met—if you live in a small apartment in a city, you may want to reconsider getting a large, high-energy dog who requires lots of exercise and space to run around in. Of course, there are exceptions (a determined new pet parent can find a way), but it's important to think this through in advance.

Do You Have Children?

Bringing a dog into your home can be one of the best things you ever do for your children—it teaches them how to care for another being and also provides them with the most loyal, loving friend. However, take into account your child's age and personality as well as the size, age, and temperament of the dog. You don't want a situation where either might get hurt. Also, always keep in mind that a dog will most certainly be *your* responsibility, not your child's. There's more on children and dogs on page 54, chapter 3.

Are Other Animals Living in the House?

Plenty of dogs live in harmony with other pets in the house—even cats. We'll address how to introduce the newcomer to the existing pets on page 55, chapter 3. At this point, if you already have a pet, think about how he's going to handle the new addition.

Is Now the Right Time?

If you're starting a new job, going through a divorce, moving, having a baby, or experiencing any other major life change, ask yourself whether you have the time and patience to care for a dog right now. You may want to wait until life calms down a bit.

Is Anyone in Your Family Allergic to Dogs?

Figure this out ahead of time by going to a friend's house with a dog similar to the one you're considering to determine any allergies. The good news is that just because someone has an allergy in your family that doesn't mean you can't get a dog. I'll explain your options later in this chapter.

Why Are You Getting a Dog?

Are you looking for a watchdog, a surrogate baby, or a best friend for your child or another dog you already have? Do you want a pet that will follow you around all day and snuggle next to you on the couch at night, or do you prefer one that likes his space? Are you planning on taking your dog on your six-mile run every morning, or do you want one that just requires a few quick walks? Figuring this out ahead of time will help you choose a dog wisely.

Is Everyone in Your Home Ready for a Pet?

If your child puts "puppy" at the top of his Christmas list, but you're not gung ho about getting a dog, then it's best to not jump the gun. The person who would spend the most time caring for the dog needs to make the final decision.

Have You Thought About the Future?

Many dogs live for ten years or much longer, so think about your future: Are you planning on moving? Getting married? Having kids? Heading to graduate school? Of course, we don't always know what the future holds, but it's smart to think about whether a dog will fit into your life for years to come.

HOW TO CHOOSE THE BEST DOG FOR YOU

Once you determine that you're definitely ready for a dog and capable of caring for one, then it's time to narrow down your choices. While some people know exactly what kind of dog they want and where to find him, others have no clue. Either way, I'll walk you through the most important issues to consider.

Puppy or Adult Dog?

It's a no-brainer why a lot of people want a puppy—they're one of the cutest creatures on earth, and there are advantages to getting your dog at this stage of his life. For starters, you're in a position to teach your pet from day one. You can prevent habits you don't like from emerging in the first place, and you can take measures to prevent your dog from having socialization issues later on in life. Of course, there's also something magical about caring for another living being from a very young age.

However, keep in mind that puppies are a lot of work, and the time commitment is huge. A puppy is brand-new to this world and knows nothing of human culture and expectations. Puppies don't come housetrained, and you have to walk them *very* often. They haven't yet learned that they're not supposed to play bite. Plus, you have to constantly monitor their every move—puppies are extremely curious and often love to chew everything in sight, so if you let your guard down they can damage your home or, worse, get hurt. In short, you'll need to be extra tolerant and patient for some time.

What are the advantages to adopting an adult dog? They don't play bite as much, and housetraining is a little less difficult simply because their bladders are more developed and they can "hold it" longer. Some dogs may even come fully housetrained and know basic requests such as "sit" and "stay." Older dogs typically cost less to acquire, too. Also, keep in mind that some of the best dogs in the world are those who have spent years in rescue shelters waiting for the perfect home.

However, there may be some disadvantages: Many older dogs may not have been socialized properly as puppies, which can make them less confident in certain situations. For example, many dogs fear men simply because they weren't exposed to them at a young age. Bad habits like destructive chewing, jumping on people, and pulling on a leash are likely more established, which means it may take a little more effort to put a stop to them.

Weigh the pros and cons of having a puppy versus an older dog and remember not to underestimate the commitment a young puppy requires. However, if you have the time and patience to dedicate to a dog regardless of his age, then either can be a perfect addition to your family.

Does Size Matter?

Some people want only a dog they can tote around in their purse; others believe that bigger is better. I've worked with dogs of all shapes and sizes, and I've learned that size has absolutely nothing to do with the personality of a dog. However, it's definitely something you should consider. Here's what you need to know:

- **Large dogs may require more room to exercise.** This is a generalization, but it's often true.

- **Smaller dogs tend to have longer life spans.** For instance, a Chihuahua can live eighteen years, whereas a Bernese Mountain Dog's life expectancy is a mere six to nine years.[2] In fact, a study published in the *American Naturalist* found that for every 4.4-pound increase in weight, life expectancy dropped by one month.[3] Of course, many variables will affect a dog's life span; size is just one of them.

- **The larger the dog, the higher the costs for his basic care.** While a small breed might eat about a half cup of kibble daily, a large one can go through ten times that. Grooming, toys, and other expenses can cost more, too.

- **Smaller dogs are more portable.** You can more easily pick them up and take them in the car or on errands. Also, on most commercial airlines, you can bring a small dog on board as a carry-on as long as he fits in a travel case under the seat in front of you.

- **Large dogs can ward off strangers.** A Bullmastiff sitting in your front window is going to scare off potential burglars more than a Maltese might, simply because of his appearance. (Though a small dog who's attentive and likes to bark can also make for an excellent watchdog.)

- **Small dogs are easier to control.** I'm not saying that it's easier to train a small dog. However, when a ten-pound dog jumps up or lunges on his leash, it's quite different from handling an eighty-pound dog with the same behavioral issues. Think about whether you have the strength to control a bigger dog.

Mixed Breed or Purebred?

People often fixate on a particular breed, but I've got to say that many of the friendliest, smartest, most capable dogs I've ever worked with were mixed breeds. These dogs, often found in shelters, are typically results of random or unintentional breeding, and they tend to cost much less than purebred dogs. (We're not talking about "designer dogs" here. I'll get to that in a second.)

On the flip side, it's understandable that many people want a particular breed. Maybe they adore Pugs because they grew up with them or German Shepherds because they make them feel safe. Also, there's the obvious advantage: with a purebred, you can safely estimate the future size, grooming needs, and appearance of your dog. With a mixed breed puppy, you can take a guess, but you might be surprised when the dog you thought was nonshedding and destined to top out at ten pounds winds up leaving hair all over the house and weighing so much you can't lift him.

Many experts argue that mixed breeds are healthier because of what's known as hybrid vigor: by combining two different breeds, you are pooling from a larger range of traits, so the dog will less likely carry one of the genetic conditions common in certain breeds. However, a large study in the *Journal of the American Veterinary Medical Association* found that the prevalence of certain genetic disorders among purebreds versus mixed breeds greatly depends on the specific health condition.[4]

Bottom line: I can't recommend one type of dog over another—for every great mixed breed there's an equally amazing purebred. And more research needs to be done on this topic before we definitively know whether one is healthier than the other. Just rest assured that with so many choices, you are sure to find a loving, well-behaved companion.

DESIGNER DOGS

You might wonder about "designer dogs" such as Cockapoos and Morkies. These dogs are mixed breeds with a twist—they're the result of intentional breeding of two purebreds to create a new breed that theoretically combines the best traits of both parents. For instance, a Cockapoo is a cross between a Cocker Spaniel and a Poodle, while a Morkie is a cross between a Maltese and a Yorkie. These puppies sometimes have a much heftier price tag than purebreds.

The popularity of these dogs has dramatically increased since the late 1980s, when an Australian breeder named Wally Conron set out to create a nonshedding Seeing Eye dog. He crossed a Labrador Retriever with a Poodle and voilà: the Labradoodle was invented, and a new trend in the dog world was launched.

Some experts claim these dogs are healthier because of hybrid vigor, though no studies have proven that. However, keep in mind a lot of these designer dogs come from puppy mills and backyard breeders who are looking to make a quick buck and have no concern for the puppy's health or temperament. In fact, according to an article in *Psychology Today*, Conron himself said, "I opened a Pandora's box, that's what I did. I released a Frankenstein. So many people are just breeding for the money. So many of these dogs have physical problems, and a lot of them are just crazy."[5]

I'm not saying you should avoid these dogs. Just don't believe all the hype. Designer dogs aren't that different from the mixes you see at a shelter. Regardless of any benefits their sellers claim, you still won't know exactly what you're going to wind up with, as temperament, appearance, and coat can vary greatly from one dog to another. Many dogs bred not to shed actually do.

CHOOSING A BREED

If you choose a purebred dog over a mutt, then your next step will be to pick a particular breed. *I can't stress enough how dangerous it can be to focus too much on breed.* People choose breeds based on stereotypes and are very often disappointed when their dog doesn't behave as he's "supposed to." However, almost no individual dog will meet all of the characteristics defined by a breed description.

Trust me: you simply cannot reliably assign attributes to your individual dog based on his breed. I've known lots of retrievers who don't retrieve, tiny Yorkies who excel at competitive Frisbee, hyper Basset Hounds, and Border Collies who were terrified of the sheep they were bred to herd.

I'm not saying to ignore breed altogether. Of course, there *are* characteristics of certain breeds that remain true: things like shedding and size are not going to vary widely, so these generalizations are more accurate. Also, if you're picking out a dog, it's still a good idea to get a wide-angle view of what certain breeds were bred to do, and if you need a dog to, say, herd cattle, then you should probably stick with a herding breed. When I first got into competitive Frisbee competitions, I purposely chose a Border Collie because I knew they are often high-energy dogs with relentless focus and physical stamina. In my dog Venus's case, she fit the stereotype in those respects, and we won many competitions. However, I know plenty of other Border Collies who wouldn't have been suited for the competitions at all.

In sum, it's fine to use breed stereotypes in a very preliminary way to get traction on the decision-making process as long as you understand that these are tentative guidelines, not absolute truths. Just as every human within a certain race, religion, or culture is different, the same concept applies to dogs: *You need to get to know the individual.*

Breed Overview

The American Kennel Club (AKC) recognizes 189 breeds and divides them into seven major dog groups based on what they were bred to do. Remember, these are generalizations—for every "rule" there's an exception. Some dogs will largely fit their stereotype, while others won't at all. Also, it's worth noting that the AKC is not the final word on what constitutes a "breed," either. There are a number of breeds not recognized by the AKC. This doesn't make them less valid. Here's a breakdown of the major dog groups:

Sporting Group: Bred to help hunters flush and retrieve game from water or land, this group includes spaniels, retrievers, pointers, and setters. They can be very active and alert, and they often require a lot of exercise.

Herding Group: This group was bred to herd other animals such as livestock. Many dogs in this group, such as the German Shepherd, Border Collie, and Welsh Corgi, are intelligent and often easily trainable.

Working Group: These dogs, such as the Rottweiler, Great Dane, Siberian Husky, and Portuguese Water Dog, were bred to guard livestock, pull sleds, and rescue. They are often intelligent, strong dogs.

Terrier Group: Bred to hunt and kill vermin, these dogs—ranging from the West Highland and Jack Russell to the Airedale and Miniature Schnauzer—can be feisty and relentless. They often have lively personalities and may make for an engaging pet.

Toy Group: Bred for companionship, these dogs—which range from the Maltese and Havanese to the Shih Tzu and Chihuahua—are small in size. They're known as lap dogs (though I've met plenty of eighty-pound dogs who think they are lap dogs, too).

Hound Group: Including dogs such as Beagles, Basset Hounds, and Dachshunds, this sturdy, diverse group was bred to assist hunters. Some may have a keen sense of smell; others may have extraordinary speed and stamina or other characteristics that help them hunt.

Non-Sporting Group: This is the group that includes all the dogs who don't seem to fit into other groups, such as the Poodle, Shar-Pei, Bichon Frise, and the Bulldog. Their size, appearance, and personality traits run the gamut.

WHERE TO FIND YOUR DOG

After you've done your research, it's time to start searching for your perfect pet. Here's where to look.

Shelters/Rescue Groups

You want a puppy? A purebred? Possibly both? No matter what kind of dog you're searching for, first look at shelters or rescue groups, which are volunteer-run organizations that sometimes focus on one breed and usually use foster families to care for dogs until they find permanent homes. You'll be amazed by the dogs you can find. According to the Humane Society of the United States (HSUS), 25 percent of dogs in shelters are purebreds.[6] As for puppies, many dogs living in these places are pregnant, and their offspring will need homes, too. Also, when pet store puppies don't sell, the stores may ship them off to shelters. You can get, say, a four-month-old puppy for less than one-tenth the price you would have paid if you had gotten the same exact dog in a pet store one month earlier.

Dogs arrive in these places for different reasons, ranging from being abandoned on the side of the road to being dropped off by loving people who couldn't care for their pet anymore because of an illness or death in the family. Some people give up their pets because of an unexpected allergy or because their new landlord doesn't allow dogs. Others decide they don't like a particular behavior, such as barking or potty accidents, and they don't want to dedicate the time to teach their dogs.

It's worth noting that, because of their backgrounds, some shelter or rescue dogs may have trust issues or difficulty interacting with, say, certain people or other animals. That's not to say that these issues can't be worked out, but you might just need a little extra time and patience socializing your dog (see page 61, chapter 3). Also, in many instances a rescued dog's past is unknown. However, unless the dog just arrived in the shelter or rescue organization that day, the staff or volunteers should be able to clue you in to the dog's personality as much as possible.

There are so many benefits to rescuing a dog. First, you know you are providing a home to an animal who is truly in need, and you're possibly saving his life. The cost of the dog is minimal compared to getting one at a breeder or pet store, and in most cases your pet will come vaccinated, microchipped, dewormed, and spayed or neutered, saving you hundreds of dollars, even more. Also, you can find a really special pet—some of the greatest dogs I've ever worked with came from shelters and rescue groups.

Visit your local shelter and also check out www.theshelterpetproject .org and www.petfinder.com, excellent sites that will help you find a shelter or rescue dog in your area. The AKC also provides a rescue network.[7] Keep in mind that new animals come into shelters and rescue groups every day, so if you don't find the dog of your dreams right away, keep checking back.

Breeders

If you have a specific need or desire for a puppy that's a particular breed, then a breeder may be for you. Some breeders are very educated about dog breeding, and they have extremely high standards and know how to breed for health and temperament. They care about the dogs they mate; often they are their beloved pets.

However, you still need to be wary—there are lots of unethical breeders out there. Some breed dogs strictly to make money and have little to no concern about the welfare of the dogs they're breeding or the health of the puppies they're selling. Others are amateurs who mate two dogs because they enjoy the hobby and want to bring in a little extra income. They may mean well but don't know much, if anything, about how to breed healthy puppies.

So how do you sort through the thousands of breeders out there to find a reputable one? Your first step is to ask people you trust—whether that be a friend who knows a lot about dogs or your local vet—for the names of breeders they recommend. Never purchase a dog off the Internet or from classified ads, as those puppies almost always come from puppy mills or irresponsible breeders. Instead, always visit a prospective breeder and see the puppies in person.

HSUS offers some more signs of a reputable breeder:[8]

- Lets you see their premises and meet the puppy's mother and, if possible, the father.

- Doesn't always have puppies for sale.

- Gives you the puppy's vaccination schedule, information on the breed, and proof that they screened the parents for breed-related health issues such as heritable cataracts and orthopedic conditions. You should also ask for proof that the dog was treated and examined by a licensed vet.

- Asks *you* a lot of questions. They won't sell their puppies to just anyone.

- Never permits puppies younger than eight weeks old to go home with you.

- Treats their breeding dogs humanely, giving the animals plenty of space to exercise, a clean environment, fresh food, water, and love.

- Happily provides references if you ask for them.

ASK *Zak*

My clients ask me tons of questions on social media. In each chapter, I'll share with you the ones I most commonly hear!

Pet Stores

"I fell in love with the cutest puppy at my local pet store, and I'm thinking of buying him. Any reason I shouldn't?"

There are many reasons. First of all, doing so supports a business that's very unethical for the most part: almost all dogs sold at pet stores come from puppy mills. This type of commercialized breeding needs to stop, and the fastest way to make that happen is to avoid getting your dog from a pet store. (One exception: Stores that specifically partner with shelters, rescue organizations, or other animal control facilities to offer dogs for adoption rather than selling commercially raised puppies.)

Dogs at mills often live their entire lives in wire cages that are cramped and filthy; many don't receive enough food, water, socialization, or veterinary care, and they sometimes never breathe fresh air or see sunlight. They can't play or exercise, and often they lose paws or limbs that get stuck in the cages or become infected. In some cases, dogs are kept outside and have to brave the harsh elements with no protection. Females are bred as much as possible without a break, and they are sometimes killed when they're done having litters. The males may also be killed when the puppy millers are done breeding them.

Once the puppies are born, they don't receive proper medical care or socialization. Due to the poor breeding conditions, these dogs often wind up with a myriad of health problems, leaving new pet parents with hefty veterinarian bills. They can have behavioral issues as well: "After leaving their mothers, puppies often spend the next several weeks or months either in transit to the broker or sitting in a cage in the pet store waiting to be sold, rather than receiving socialization from their parent and littermates and from a human family," says Kathleen Summers, director of outreach and research for the Puppy Mills Campaign of HSUS. Because they miss this crucial period of socialization, these puppies can become shy, anxious, and aggressive. In fact, a study in the *Journal of the American Veterinary Medical Association* found that when compared with puppies from noncommercial sources, puppies from pet stores were more aggressive and fearful and they had more separation anxiety and difficulty housetraining.[9]

People are taking a stand against puppy mills. More than seventy different localities in the United States have put laws in place to outlaw pet stores from selling puppies. Also, HSUS has started the Puppy-Friendly Pet Stores Initiative, which asks pet stores to stop selling commercially raised puppies and instead offer pets for adoption from local shelters or sell only supplies. About 2,300 pet stores have made the pledge so far.

I'm not saying you can't find a great dog at a pet store, but the odds *are* stacked against you. And why support puppy mills when millions of great puppies and adult dogs enter shelters every year? For those of you who have already gotten a dog from a pet store, know that you did give that dog a better life by getting him out of a cage (or crib!) and into your home. However, because of the reasons I've just explained, if you ever decide to get another dog in the future, stick with a shelter, a rescue group, or a responsible breeder.

Allergies

"I think I'm allergic to dogs. Can I still get one anyway?"

This depends on the severity of the allergies and how much you love dogs! I've known plenty of people who adopt dogs despite their allergies to them. Many are willing to make the trade-off; others aren't. It's a personal decision.

About 15 to 30 percent of people with allergies are allergic to dogs—specifically to their dander (flakes of dead skin), urine, or saliva.[10] Despite popular belief, no particular type of dog is truly hypoallergenic. A study in the *American Journal of Rhinology & Allergy* found that people who live with breeds that are purportedly hypoallergenic have the same amount of dog allergens in their homes as do people who live with dogs known not to be hypoallergenic.[11] One individual dog might cause allergies in one person, while a different dog can cause allergies in another. According to the Asthma and Allergy Foundation of America, some symptoms of a dog allergy include coughing; shortness of breath and wheezing; watery, red, or itchy eyes; sneezing; a skin rash; and a runny or stuffy nose. People with asthma and other allergies can have particularly severe reactions. Talk with your doctor about skin or blood tests that can help determine whether or not you're truly allergic to dogs. If you are, but you just can't live without a furry friend, you can still take steps to protect yourself:

- Keep your dog out of your bedroom and off furniture if possible.

- Wash your hands with soap and water after petting or hugging your dog.

- Invest in a high-efficiency particulate air (HEPA) cleaner.

- Use a high-efficiency vacuum cleaner or a central vacuum to limit allergen levels.

- Wipe down your dog regularly with a damp cloth or wipes to remove dander and loose hairs. (Talk to your vet about how often to bathe your dog, based on your pet's coat.)

- Discuss possible allergy treatments with your doctor.

Pit Bulls

"Everyone tells me to avoid rescuing a Pit Bull because they are violent and dangerous dogs. Is that true?"

No other dog breed has fallen victim to stereotypes as much as Pit Bulls have. I've worked with hundreds of these dogs, and almost all of them were sweet, loving, and highly intelligent. None were any more aggressive than other breeds I've encountered. People think they are more challenging and difficult to train, but Pit Bulls and other breeds or mixes that people deem "dangerous"—such as Akitas, Rottweilers, German Shepherds, Chow Chows, and Doberman Pinschers—can be some of the best dogs around.

You'll hear stories in the media about the dangers of Pit Bulls, but those news reports fail to explain that violence involving these dogs has more to do with the type of person who gravitates toward these breeds than the dogs themselves. In fact, a study in the *Journal of Interpersonal Violence* found that people who have "high-risk" breeds such as Pit Bulls have ten times as many criminal convictions as those who had "lower-risk" breeds.[12] Some people may exploit dogs by training them to fight or be aggressive. (A loving pet parent like you isn't going to do that!) Another study in the *Journal of the American Veterinary Medical Association* examined dog bite–related fatalities and found that breed was not a factor.[13] For such reasons, the Centers for Disease Control and Prevention, the American Veterinary Society of Animal Behavior, and many other organizations have publicly opposed breed-specific legislation, as it doesn't help reduce dog bite incidents and deaths.[14] Also, experts point out that if certain breeds such as Pit Bulls are regulated, people with violent or irresponsible tendencies will simply find another breed to manipulate.

Such statistics haven't stopped people from believing what they want to believe. Breed-specific legislation still exists in the United States that bans or restricts Pit Bulls and other breeds. Great Britain has banned Pit Bulls and certain other dogs altogether.[15] Luckily, some of these laws have been overturned, but we have a long way to go. Hopefully, with education, more good people will learn the truth about Pit Bulls and consider bringing them into their homes.

Remember that there certainly are aggressive Pit Bulls, but there are also aggressive Chihuahuas and Golden Retrievers. Evaluate Pit Bulls as you would any other breed. If you do decide you want one of these dogs, Pit Bulls are extremely common in shelters and rescue groups, so these are the ideal places to go to have your "pick of the litter," often including puppies.

Traveling

"I travel for work about once a month and often take weekend getaways with friends, but I really want to get a dog. Can a person with my lifestyle make it work?"

I usually suggest that people in this position strongly consider whether a dog is right for them, but if you're willing to board your dog at a reputable daycare center, ask a friend or family member to help out, or hire a well-vetted pet sitter, then go for it! When I had to travel overseas to film my second TV series, *Who Let the Dogs Out?*, I hired and trained my cousin Mark to watch my dogs and exercise them. He took such good care of them, I'm sure they barely missed me! It's particularly important that your dog stays on his routine while you are gone in order to minimize stress and the likelihood that unwanted behaviors will emerge.

Male or Female?

"I'm trying to decide whether to choose a male or a female dog. What are the pros and cons of either gender?"

When selecting a dog, there are so many other factors to consider that are more important than gender. You really need to find the individual that you connect with. However, I know that lots of people strongly prefer one gender of dog to the other. The battle of the sexes certainly doesn't just apply to humans! Some might say that male dogs are more affectionate, while female dogs are more independent. Others say males are goofy and playful, while females are easier to train. And then there's the expression you'll hear from people in the dog industry: "If you want a good dog, get a male. If you want a great dog, get a female and cross your fingers."

We really need to move away from this line of thinking. Assigning traits to male dogs and female dogs is like saying all girls like to play with Barbie dolls and wear pink while all boys prefer playing with toy cars and throwing a ball around. We've come so far fighting these stereotypes in humans; it's time we do the same with dogs. Also, there are no studies that back up these gender qualities you may hear about; they're all anecdotal. I've worked with thousands of dogs in my career and have witnessed many personality traits in both sexes.

However, there are a few things to consider. While most people should get their dogs spayed or neutered as soon as possible, some may opt to wait for various reasons. In those cases, keep in mind that unspayed female dogs will go into heat approximately twice a year, during which time they'll have a blood-tinged vaginal discharge. This can be messy and will also attract male dog attention, so you'll need to keep an extra watchful eye on your dog when you're in public. Unneutered male dogs may exhibit marking behavior (though female dogs may mark, too). Also, if you want a particular breed and size or strength matters to you, then know that males tend to be stronger and heavier compared to females of the same breed.

Lastly, a note if you are adding a second dog to your family: while in my experience dogs who live together usually get along, I have seen that most cases of interdog aggression in a household involve same-sex pairs. A study in the *Journal of the American Veterinary Medical Association* found the same thing.[16] I don't want to dissuade you from adding, say, a male dog to your house if you already have another male dog because in the majority of cases you should be fine. It's just something to consider.

FINDING "THE ONE"

You've done your research. Maybe you've really homed in on a particular breed. Possibly your only criteria is finding a puppy who won't get bigger than ten pounds. Or you could just be looking for a companion who will have certain traits—a dog who'll sit by your feet all day while you work or one that will happily join you on a long hike.

Well, now comes the fun part—it's time to choose your dog! I recommend spending a good hour or two with the dogs who make your short list of criteria at the local shelter, rescue organization, or breeder. Meet lots of dogs and find the one you click with.

For instance, when my coauthor Dina decided to add a second dog to her family, she went to a local animal shelter to see if she might find the right one. She walked in and immediately noticed this scrappy white ball of fuzz with a spotted belly. All the dogs were jumping and barking in excitement, but as soon as this one saw her he wagged his tail and stared at her with a pair of the sweetest, most soulful eyes. She said she probably could have ended her search right there, but she asked the animal care worker to bring that puppy, along with four others who fit her basic criteria, into the communal area so she could interact with them and watch them play. All the dogs ran around and chased each other, but that white dog eventually sat down next to Dina, looked up at her with those eyes, and placed his paw on her leg. She said it was as though he was saying "Please. Pick me." Well, that was it. She brought him home to join her family the very next day. His name is Brody.

That story highlights some of the key things you should do when choosing your dog:

Determine Energy Level

Energy level is far and away the single most important factor to think about when considering a prospective dog. It's the easiest way to categorize whether or not a dog is right for you. For example, once an older couple came into one of my training classes with a toy breed dog who was off the charts with energy. I would rather have seen these guys with a low-energy dog (even a mellow Border Collie!) than the little guy they came in with. It's not that the *breed* was wrong for them, but the dog's *energy* certainly was.

So how do you choose a dog based on energy level? Here I've outlined the different levels so you can figure out where a dog fits. However, keep in mind that when first meeting many dogs, their energy is likely to be very high due to the excitement of greeting someone new. Make sure you ask the breeder or shelter worker what the energy level of the prospective dog is like during his downtime. Also, try to visit the dog multiple times to get a more complete sense of what his personality is like.

ENERGY LEVEL ONE: LOW

Description: Because these dogs lie around most of the time, they make a great companion for a relatively inactive person. These couch potatoes require a few short daily walks, and then they're happy snuggling next to you for the rest of the day. Low-energy dogs are not typically motivated to learn very advanced tasks, nor are they likely to be impressive athletes. However, they'll likely make up for it in good behavior, and you won't have to put in as much effort to train them as you would need to for a higher-energy dog.

What to Look For: Untrained level one dogs may wag their tails and come up to you, but they're usually not the type to incessantly jump all over you. Look for the dog who interacts with people and other dogs but does not engage in sustained, vigorous play. When considering a dog who seems to be a level one, first make sure that you rule out sickness or a recent change in the dog's environment as the cause of his calmness. That way when you get home you won't be in for any surprises—like finding out that the dog is actually a little Energizer bunny!

ENERGY LEVEL TWO: MODERATE

Description: Level two dogs are mellow most of the time, but they will have bursts of energy. They are great for the person who wants a hands-on role in training and teaching; these dogs are good at almost everything, though they may not be perfect at anything. If you want a dog to go running with or to play with at the park, but you're not looking for exceptional physical talent, then one of these may be your best choice. Most people will do very well with a level two dog.

What to Look For: When you first meet an untrained level two dog, you are likely to encounter some jumping. Don't be turned off by this, as a dog who jumps or seems a bit pushy is simply a dog who wants to interact with you. That is a very good thing! These dogs typically enjoy socializing and playing casual or even sustained games of chase with other dogs. They may also have occasional periods of barking or racing around the house, but they'll calm down fairly naturally after five to ten minutes without a ton of encouragement from you.

ENERGY LEVEL THREE: HIGH

Description: Without regular exercise, these dogs are always raring to go; they can play all day and night. Generally speaking, the higher energy a dog has, the more teachable he is. You'd be shocked by what some level three dogs can learn. I'm talking riding bikes, walking on their front paws, and leaping off docks without fear! However, you've got to dedicate a lot of time to making sure these dogs get plenty of mental and physical exercise—if you don't, all that pent-up energy can lead to destructive behaviors, and training can become very challenging. These dogs are typically best for a person who has the time and energy to commit to some serious training.

What to Look For: Look for the dog who runs up to you and either jumps like crazy or insists that you play tug-of-war or fetch by constantly bringing you a toy. That's probably an untrained level three dog! These dogs will usually have a tail that wags at a hundred miles an hour. They may stare at you enthusiastically as though they're saying, "Let's play!" Also, they seem to never tire and will engage with you as long as you're willing. Put a lot of thought into whether or not a level three dog is right for you, as they are generally the highest maintenance of all dogs.

Meet the Parents

The expression "The apple doesn't fall far from the tree" applies to dogs, too. Like people, dogs often inherit personality traits from their parents. If possible, observe the mother and father of a dog you're considering; this may give you a ballpark idea of what the dog may be like when he is older. Better yet, ask the person who knows these dogs best as much as you can about them. Of course, in many cases you won't be able to find out anything about a dog's parents. However, in the case of a puppy bred by a reputable breeder or one born in a shelter, you should be able to learn some helpful information.

Remember First Impressions

As a dog trainer, I've been surprised to learn that dogs' personalities really don't seem to change from when they're puppies. There are no doubt exceptions, but in general what you see *is* what you get. So if there's one puppy in a litter that seems very pushy, energetic, or mischievous, chances are he'll always have at least a bit of that in him. One that snuggles right up to you and gives you lots of kisses? I bet he'll always be a sweetie.

Look at the Eyes

The eyes and overall demeanor of a dog give you the most accurate depiction of his personality and mind-set at that moment. Ask yourself during the evaluation process, "What does it look like this dog is saying?" Are his eyes big and wide, combined with a wiggly butt and wagging tail? Then this is probably a friendly dog who desperately wants to interact with you. Or, when you gaze into his eyes, does he look away and lie down? This could be a shyer dog. Maybe the dog's eyes suggest that he is indifferent to your presence. Such behavior can suggest maturity and heavy socialization where the presence of a new person is a common occurrence. (Please note: I'm *not* saying that when evaluating a dog you should stare him down—a dog might possibly misinterpret that as a sign of intimidation.)

Ask a Lot of Questions

It can sometimes be difficult to determine if a dog fits your criteria after spending, say, thirty minutes to an hour with one at a shelter or breeder. Here's where the breeder or shelter worker can help. Some might have even done what's known as a temperament test, which helps evaluate the puppy or dog even further by seeing how he reacts in certain situations. (These tests may include questions such as: Does he startle easily? How does he handle being cradled? Will he fetch or follow you if you have a toy?) If so, ask these experts about the results and what they might mean for that particular dog.

Consider Further Testing

There are other personality indicators to look for when considering a dog. Does the dog seem eager to interact with you when you reach your hand out, or does he back away? If a dog tries to engage in playful activity, he is likely to be generally accepting of you and strangers. However, if his tail goes between his legs or he hides under a table, then these may be signs of a dog who is nervous or anxious. If you're the patient type, don't overlook these dogs—once you achieve a bond with them, not only will you be able to help them become more confident through sufficient socialization, but they'll also trust you and love you like no other.

You can also check for teachability by bringing a squeaky toy with you. A dog's fascination with a squeaky toy indicates curiosity, which is related to intelligence. Keep in mind that if the dog seems to want to play with the toy for hours, that may mean you have a very high-energy dog on your hands, one who will require a lot of training to be manageable. Conversely, a dog who shows little interest in a squeaky toy is more likely to be a lower-energy dog and lower maintenance.

Next, see whether a dog follows a lure. Lure training is where you use a tiny piece of really good food, like real chicken, to coax your dog into a specific position like "sit" or "lie down." If a dog follows a lure eagerly, this is also a good sign that he will take to intermediate or even advanced training when the time comes. So when you first meet a dog, ask his current caretaker if you can give him a small treat—then use that lure to see if you can get the dog to follow you. We'll cover lure training in depth on page 125, chapter 6, but for now your goal is to see if a dog will stay focused on a treat as you firmly hold it and slowly move it up and down and side to side.

Go Slowly

Take your time making sure that the dog you bring home is the right one for *you*. By considering all the issues we've gone over in this chapter, you'll be giving your new family member the best start possible.

CHAPTER TWO

BEFORE YOUR DOG COMES HOME: EVERYTHING YOU NEED TO PREPARE FOR YOUR PET'S ARRIVAL

Few things are as exciting as bringing a new dog home. However, it's also natural to feel overwhelmed in the first few weeks or even months. Your dog has a lot to learn, and you have a lot to teach! One way to ease your pet's homecoming is by getting ready *before* her arrival, which is exactly what this chapter will help you do. You wouldn't bring a baby home without having diapers, a car seat, bottles, and clothing on hand, right? You'd possibly have also painted the nursery and set up the crib, and you'd likely have a pediatrician's number taped to your fridge or added to your phone.

Well, it's important to think much the same way about a dog. That way when she first pads through your front door, you can relax, knowing your house is safe and stocked with everything you may need to care for her. You'll also have some of the logistics worked out. In turn, your dog will adapt faster to her new surroundings as she realizes that she's now in a place where she'll be loved and protected.

SHOPPING LIST:
WHAT TO BUY FOR YOUR NEW DOG

By stocking up on some essentials before your dog arrives, you'll help make sure she stays healthy and happy as she eases into her new home. Here are some essentials you'll want to get (other than paper towels, of course!):

❑ **Dog Crate**

The biggest mistake new pet parents sometimes make is not sufficiently controlling the environment of their new dog. A dog crate can be a convenient way to help you do just that for short periods. Most dogs love it, provided you introduce it correctly and make the crate an enjoyable place to be. Crates not only provide dogs with a sense of safety but also help keep them secure when you're out of the house or too occupied to watch them. Another bonus: Dogs don't like to soil where they sleep, so crates help greatly with housetraining.

Durable plastic crates are easy to clean and perfect for traveling. Wire crates are another option—they offer more ventilation and a full view, and you can cover them with a towel at night to create a cozier atmosphere. Look for a crate that is easy to open and close and large enough that your dog can stand up and turn around in it easily. If your crate is much larger than that, a dog may initially soil one end but not the other until she realizes that her *whole* crate is her bedroom. (Just keep in mind that when it comes to the size of a crate, too big is always better than too small.) You might also consider getting an oversized crate with an adjustable divider panel so that you can slowly expand the room your dog has as she grows and also begins to understand that she shouldn't do her business in the crate. See page 59, chapter 3, and page 100, chapter 5, for more information on crate training.

❏ Baby Gate and Puppy Playpen

A gate and a playpen can come in handy and assist you with the supervision process. A gate prevents your dog from entering rooms you don't want her to go into, while a playpen allows her to run around and play in a confined area. Gates are also essential for blocking staircases—dogs can fall down stairs and wind up with serious injuries. Keep one up until your dog is at least six months old and can navigate the stairs on her own.

A gate and a playpen are also great options if you don't want to use a crate for any reason. When choosing a gate, find one that's durable and made of a material other than wood. Make sure no openings on the gate are large enough for the dog to stick her head through—she can wind up getting stuck or strangled. As for a playpen, make sure it is sturdy and that your dog can't chew through it or climb out of it.

❏ Bowls

Your dog will need at least one bowl for food and one for water. Get a few extras so that you can wash them every day and easily swap out a dirty water bowl with a clean one. Stainless steel is your best bet because it's durable and won't chip. Heavy ceramic is another option, but make sure it doesn't contain lead, which can be toxic to your dog. Avoid anything with dyes, and stay away from plastic if possible—some dogs are allergic to it. Others like to chew on the plastic, and such bowls can splinter off into tiny pieces that your dog might swallow. Also, if you have a dog with long ears, such as hounds and spaniels, look for bowls that are specially tapered so her ears don't get wet or dirty while she eats.

❏ Food

Find out what your dog has been eating at the place where you found her and buy a small bag of that food. Suddenly switching from one food to another can cause diarrhea (just what you need with a dog who isn't housetrained yet!). Chapter 3 addresses how to switch food when you're ready; chapter 8 helps you pick the best food for your pet.

❏ Identification

If your dog were to run away and get lost, an ID tag that hooks onto your dog's collar can be the key to reuniting with her. It's up to you what the tag says; at least include your phone number so if someone finds your dog, they can contact you. Some people opt to also include their name, address, their dog's name, and other identifying details.

❏ A Collar or Harness

Your dog will need a collar right away to hold her ID tag and eventually her rabies tag. At first, just pick up a simple adjustable nylon or leather collar that buckles together. (Save the receipt in case it doesn't fit.) It shouldn't be too tight, but it also shouldn't be so loose that it'll slip right off—you should be able to slip only two fingers under the collar. Take the collar off when your dog is in her crate—she may scratch at it until she gets used to it, and her foot could get stuck in it. The collar itself can also get stuck on the crate, creating a choking risk. While a collar is essential for your dog's ID tags, a harness is also great for most dogs for general control, safety, and training—especially for puppies eight months and younger, small breeds, those with short noses such as Pugs and Boxers, and dogs with thin necks such as Greyhounds. Choose one that's easy to get on and off. Another consideration: If your dog is a very young puppy or a tiny breed such as a Yorkie or a Maltese, you might want to put a small bell on her collar so people can hear when she's approaching and avoid stepping on her.

❏ Leashes

You'll need a leash not only to walk your dog but possibly also to keep her tethered to you during training. For the initial leash, choose one that's four to six feet long. I suggest nylon because they are the least expensive, you can tie them to a belt loop, and they are the easiest to wash, though leather and rope are fine, too. Retractable leashes are another option some people like, particularly to give their dogs some room to roam and sniff around while also maintaining control of their environment. However, when taking your dog on proper walks or in public, refrain from using a retractable leash until she's well trained. You'll also need a longer lead leash—twenty to thirty feet—for training.

❏ Grooming Tools

It's your responsibility to keep your dog clean, but which tools you'll need depends on her breed or combination of breeds and whether or not you plan to hire a groomer or do it yourself. At first, at least make sure you have a good bristle brush to keep your dog's coat tangle free. Pick up shampoo, nail trimmers, cotton balls, an ear cleaner, a toothbrush, and toothpaste. For more information on grooming supplies, see chapter 8.

❏ Toys

Bouncy balls, stuffed plush elephants, flying discs, and tug toys—the dog toys available on the market these days would give Toys"R"Us a run for its money. Don't go overboard—buy a few different types and see what your dog's preferences are. Choose toys that are durable, size-appropriate, and a little bigger than you think you need; for instance, choose a ball that will fit in your dog's mouth but one she can't swallow.

Many dogs, especially puppies, have a strong urge to chew—stick with hard rubber toys that help her satisfy this need. Also, if you notice your pet tearing her squeaky rabbit to shreds or eating the plastic eyes off of it, or a toy rope starts to fray, then remove it immediately. If your dog is an aggressive chewer, choose toys that are "indestructible," "ultra durable," or something similar.

❏ Chemical Deodorizer

When you're housetraining, your dog is going to have accidents in the house. It's a normal part of the process. Of course, you're going to clean up any mess right away, but your dog's keen sense of smell will detect the urine or feces odor for a long time even when you can't. This, in turn, can lead her to continue marking the same spot repeatedly, as at first dogs are likely to go to the same spot or two to do their business. To remove the odor, clean the soiled spot with an enzyme-based chemical deodorizer you can find in pet supply stores or some grocery stores.

❏ Poop Bags or Scooper

Many areas require by law that people pick up their dog's poop. And even if your city or neighborhood doesn't, do it anyway—leaving a mess on the street is not only unneighborly, it's also dangerous: it can cause the spread of parasites, and the feces can wash into local water sources and contaminate it. Stock up on plastic bags or pick up some waste bags at your pet supply store along with a dispenser that attaches to your dog's leash. After your dog goes potty, put the bag over your hand, grab the poop, and then turn the bag inside out and tie it closed; when you get home, dispose of it in your trash. Another option: a pooper-scooper, a device designed to pick up dog poop, handy for cleaning up your yard.

❏ Treats

Treats can be an essential training tool or just a nice way to give your dog a little something special. I recommend having two main types of treats for training. The first is high-quality soft dog treats (commonly known as "training treats") that you can store at room temperature and easily access to reward your dog spontaneously when she does something you like. However, for primary training sessions, you'll want to get your dog excited and motivated for training, so the key is to choose a treat that she really loves. I always include tiny pieces of boiled chicken or another real meat as the treat. Yes, I'm talking about the same stuff we humans eat!

In general, make sure training treats are low in fat and sodium and made in America. Also, while I don't advise over-treating your dog with low-quality commercial dog treats "just because," the occasional traditional dog biscuit is fine. Don't feed your pet jerky treats: since 2007, the Food and Drug Administration has received thousands of reports of pets becoming sick or even dying after eating jerky treats.[1] Most of these treats were made in China, but not all treat packaging indicates where they were made. Just avoid them. In fact, make it a general rule to avoid any pet food or treats from China for the time being.

❏ Bones and Rawhides

You'll likely want to have at least a bone or two on hand to help satisfy your dog's chewing urge, which is particularly strong for puppies as their teeth come in. Think big: always choose a bone that your dog can't possibly choke on. If you want to give your dog rawhides, buy the ones that are compressed and don't have a twist on the end (dogs can unwind these, which can lead to a choking hazard). Once your dog has consumed half the rawhide, replace it, and if you notice that your dog is going through rawhides very quickly, find something else for her to chew. Another favorite option: 100 percent naturally shed deer antlers, which last an extremely long time, clean teeth, and don't stain, splinter, or chip. Other hard bones that don't splinter may be good options, too.

❏ Bedding

You'll have dozens of dog beds to choose from, if and when you decide to purchase one for your pet—everything from your basic donut beds to luxury couches, orthopedic cushions, and even heated beds. But don't invest in a pricey bed right off the bat; wait until your dog is done housetraining. Also, during their first several months or even longer, many dogs (even some adult dogs) will chew up their new bed. In the meantime, you can make your dog's crate extra cozy with a simple mat or old blankets or towels (as long as she doesn't chew them).

DOG PROOFING

Your dog, particularly if she's a puppy, is like a curious toddler—she's going to want to explore everything in her new home, and she'll completely depend on you to stay safe. The best way to do that is to constantly supervise her: keep her on a leash next to you when you're home, and put her in her crate or other secure area when you can't keep an eye on her.

However, eventually your dog may explore more of your house on her own (especially during those times when you accidentally drop your guard). It's important to remember that she may take *anything* into her mouth, and it's your job to make sure she doesn't have access to things that can hurt her, from Lego pieces to food scraps. Crouch down and try to view your home through your dog's eyes. Remove or secure anything she might chew on, eat, or otherwise destroy with her inquisitive mouth. Dogs are craftier and smarter than most people imagine, so be thorough! Here's what to consider:

Electrical Cords

If a dog bites an electrical cord while it's plugged in, it not only will shock her but also can cause severe electrical burns on the corners of her mouth. Depending on the voltage, it can even electrocute her. Make sure all cords are out of your dog's reach or unplug them until you need them. Her life might depend on it.

Food

Your dog will make it her job to find any food in the house and eat it. And she won't discriminate—whether it's a few crumbs that fell on the floor or leftovers in the garbage, to her it's a four-star meal. The scary part is that many common human foods can cause symptoms ranging from vomiting and diarrhea to seizures and death.

According to the American Society for the Prevention of Cruelty to Animals (ASPCA), some of the foods most dangerous to dogs include chocolate (the darker, the more dangerous), avocado (particularly the pit), coffee, alcohol, macadamia nuts, grapes, raisins, yeast dough, moldy foods, xylitol (an artificial sweetener used in sugar-free products like gum), onions, and garlic.[2] Chicken bones can choke them. Make sure you put all food in cabinets or containers that your pet can't access, and secure your kitchen garbage pail. Also, remember that your dog is resourceful—just because she can't jump from the floor onto your kitchen table to reach a fruit bowl, that doesn't mean she won't use a nearby chair as a step stool.

Common Household Products

Put a latch on any cabinets that contain cleaning products such as bleach and laundry detergent, soaps, shampoos, insecticides, rat poison, paint, paint thinners, pool chemicals, or antifreeze. Don't keep any loose change lying around—pennies made in 1983 or later contain zinc, which is toxic to dogs. Place medication on high shelves out of reach, and if you drop a pill, make sure you find it—if your dog eats just one, say, ibuprofen, it can shut down her liver and kidneys. Also, childproof bottles are not puppy-proof—dogs can chew through them.

Houseplants and Flowers

Many common plants are toxic for dogs—ASPCA includes detailed information about which ones are safe and which ones aren't at www.aspca
.org/pet-care/animal-poison-control/toxic-and-non-toxic-plants.

Some of the common ones you should keep away from your dog include azaleas, oleanders, certain varieties of lilies, sago palm, tulips, daffodils, amaryllis, and chrysanthemums.[3] Consider *all* plants toxic until you learn otherwise, and make sure your dog can't gain access to any of them.

Toilet Bowls

Keep the lids on your toilet bowls shut at all times. Not only might dogs drink toxic cleaning chemicals in the bowl but they can also drown if they fall in.

Clothing

Check that your laundry baskets are shut tight and that your dog doesn't have access to your clothing, towels, or shoes. The fabric, buttons, or strings on these items can get stuck in a dog's intestines, causing severe vomiting and possibly requiring surgery. Also, keep all jewelry and hair ties in a drawer or case that your dog can't access.

Backyard

Ideally, you should enclose your backyard to keep your dog from running away and to prevent other animals from entering your property. However, even though a fence stops her from escaping from the yard, that doesn't mean there aren't dangers in the yard itself—along with toxic shrubbery and plants, your dog might consume acorns, palm nuts, sticks, and even rocks that she could choke on. Cocoa mulch, fertilizer, and pesticides can also be very harmful. Clear the yard of any such potential dangers if possible, and *always* keep an eye on your dog when she's out there.

Health Insurance for Your Dog

Just as in the people world, dogs' medical needs will vary throughout their lives. There will be times when your dog becomes injured or sick, and you'll have to weigh which course of action to take. It's a lot easier to make the decision that's best for your dog without having to worry about the cost. That's where health insurance comes into play.

Health insurance plans can help protect you in case, for example, your dog swallows a small toy or is hit by a car and needs immediate medical care. Such situations might require X-rays, ultrasound, surgery, and/or medication, which can rack up a bill that's $1,000 or higher. However, just like human health insurance, pet health insurance companies vary greatly in what they cover, how much they'll cover, deductibles, and various other restrictions. The key is to do your homework and, with the help of your vet, weigh the pros and cons of various plans. (TruPanion, ASPCA, and Healthy Paws are popular ones. The website www.petinsurancereview .com offers good comparisons of most companies.) Just remember that if you're going to get pet health insurance, the sooner the better—the older your dog is, the more likely preexisting conditions won't be covered.

If you don't want to get pet insurance but are worried about affording unexpected medical issues, at least start a savings account for your pet. Add a certain amount to it every month (say, $25), and don't use it for anything but major bills (regular checkups and vaccinations should be calculated in your overall budget). That way, in case the unthinkable happens to your dog, you can focus on helping her get the medical care she needs without the stress of figuring out how you're going to pay for it.

PROCEDURES YOUR DOG MIGHT HAVE BEFORE SHE COMES HOME

Of course, you're planning on taking your new dog to the vet as soon as she comes home. But your pet might have been poked and prodded, and even undergone surgery before she arrives. Some of these procedures are essential for your dog's health and well-being; others are unnecessary and potentially painful for her. Here's a breakdown:

Vaccinations
It's important that dogs are vaccinated against a whole host of viruses such as rabies, distemper, and parvovirus. Normally, the first

combination vaccine is given at six or seven weeks of age, before a puppy goes home. When you pick up your dog, make sure you get a proof of vaccination document to bring to your first vet visit. For more on vaccinations, see page 178, chapter 8.

Microchips

A microchip can save your dog's life. Each year, out of the millions of dogs who go missing, most are never reunited with their families. What's worse, many whom are found are sent to shelters and possibly euthanized. A microchip can make this less likely. A vet will inject the microchip—a permanent identification chip about the size of a grain of rice—between your dog's shoulder blades. This has no known side effects.

Once your dog is microchipped, your next step is to register with the microchip company (Home Again and Microchip ID Systems are two common examples). It's simple—you just provide your name and contact information and pay a minimal fee. That information remains in a national database.

Then, if your dog ever goes missing and is found by someone, a person at a vet's office or shelter can read the chip with a scanner and return her to you. If your new dog hasn't been microchipped before you pick her up, ask your vet to do so. Just remember that if you ever move or change your phone number, you need to contact your pet's microchip company to update that information.

Deworming

Most puppies—regardless of where they come from—pick up parasites such as roundworms, tapeworms, hookworms, and whipworms from their mothers while in utero or from nursing. This is normal but it needs to be addressed, as these parasites can give your dog anemia, bloating, diarrhea, and other gastrointestinal problems. A dog can also spread some of these parasites to humans. Usually, when a puppy is around two weeks, a vet will squirt a deworming liquid into her mouth that will kill any parasites. Your dog will need follow-up treatments again every two weeks until she is two or three months old.

Tail Docking and Ear Cropping

Tail docking is the intentional removal of part of an animal's tail. Ear cropping is the removal and shaping of an animal's earflap so it stands erect. The American Veterinary Medical Association opposes these procedures when done solely for cosmetic purposes and "encourages the elimination of ear cropping and tail docking from breed standards."[5]

Tail docking is typically done a few days after birth without anesthesia, especially for certain breeds such as spaniels and terriers. The tails are usually cut with surgical scissors and the skin around it is stitched up. This procedure is painful and can affect how a puppy perceives pain for the rest of her life.[6] Ear cropping is usually done on dogs between six to twelve weeks of age under general anesthesia. The dog's ears are cut so they point straight up, then stitched (think of breeds such as Dobermans, Schnauzers, Great Danes, and Pit Bulls).

These procedures are illegal in many countries, but still performed in the United States. You may not have any say in whether or not your puppy's tail is docked or her ears are cropped—by the time you find her, the damage may have already been done. However, if you do have a choice, I strongly advise against these unnecessary procedures.

Dewclaw Removal

Some dogs are born with an extra toe up around the ankle called a dewclaw—think of it like a human's thumb, though it serves no real purpose. Unlike tail docking and ear cropping, there are some medical reasons a person might want to have their puppy's dewclaws removed. Dewclaws can get caught on fences or carpets or become irritated while digging, or a dog can bump them into surfaces when she runs around the room. Breeders often have dewclaws removed when the puppy is a few days old. You can have your vet remove them later, but the earlier the better.

ASK *Zak*

Bringing Home a New Dog

"What's the earliest age I can safely bring home my new pet?"

No earlier than eight weeks. Sooner than that, and you may be asking for trouble. Many states have instituted puppy sale laws that dictate that puppies can't be sold before that time.[4] Up until then, a puppy still needs her mother's care. Puppies separated too early from their mother and littermates are missing out on some key socialization skills that close kinship can teach best. Also, a puppy's digestive tract is still developing, and if you bring her home too early she may not be ready to consume solid food. Lastly, keep in mind that the younger the puppy, the longer it might take to housetrain her—she simply won't be able to physically "hold it in."

Choosing a Name

"My husband wants to name our dog Betty, but I have my heart set on Snuggles. How do we decide the best name for our dog?"

Consider including all family members in this fun decision. Put a lot of thought into it—after all, you'll be saying your dog's name dozens of times each day!

You might have heard that a dog can get confused easily if her name rhymes with certain words like "sit," "come," or "down." As you'll learn by reading this book, dogs are smart and very capable of discerning the difference. Other people might say that a name should be short, while some professionals advise against human names because this may anthropomorphize your dog. These opinions are far too common in the dog world, and they're just not true.

Of course, use your best judgment. A name like Snuffleupagus is quite a mouthful, while one like Butthead is crass and shows no respect for a dog. Choose a name that's cool, fun, majestic, sentimental, or just something that you love that fits your awesome new pet.

Preparing the Family

"My family and I are so excited that our new pet is coming home next week. Is there anything I can do to get all of us ready for her arrival?"

When a dog first comes home, her world will seem upside down. She'll feel a lot more comfortable if you seem to have everything in order. Now's the time to lay out some ground rules and make sure everyone in your household is on the same page. *There is a direct correlation between how consistent you are and the results you can expect!* If you, your spouse, children, roommate, and anyone else who will have a lot of contact with your dog aren't consistent, your pet will figure out whom to listen to and whom to ignore. Some things to consider:

- Always keep your dog's safety in mind. If you have a puppy or small dog, teach your children never to leave her on a couch or bed where she can fall off and severely hurt herself. Also, allow young children to hold her only while they're sitting. Never leave a dog unattended with a small child.

- Remind everyone in the family that anything the dog can reach is something she'll potentially chew on. For instance, if the kids come home from school and throw their backpacks on the floor, the dog might sniff out their leftover lunch or any other "edibles." Also, explain to them that not only is their pet capable of destroying their possessions, such as figurines and stuffed animals, but she can also choke on them. You can't expect her to be able to differentiate between her toys and theirs at first.

- Decide who in your family will be your dog's main trainer. Then, as that person learns the individual nature of the family dog and how to effectively interact with her, she can teach the rest of the family how to do the same. That way, the dog has a primary teacher and the rest of the family members will be on the same page.

- Explain to children that the dog will need a little time to adjust to her new environment. Of course, everyone will have plenty of time to play with their new pet, but they should also understand up front that she'll need some alone time, too. Always make sure the kids are not too rough with your dog.

Choosing a Vet

"There are about a dozen veterinarians in my area. How do I know who's the right one for me and my dog?"

It's important to establish a relationship with a vet *before* your dog comes home. For one, you don't want to search desperately for a vet and make a hasty decision because your dog is in dire need of medical attention. Also, even if your new dog was checked by a vet at the place where you found her, you'll still want to have a medical professional you trust make sure your pet is healthy within forty-eight hours of bringing her home. Dogs, especially ones from shelters and puppy stores, often come home with minor illnesses due to immature immune systems and the fact that they could have caught an illness from one of the many other animals they lived with. If your dog has a cough, for instance, the vet can make sure she gets the antibiotics she needs before it turns into pneumonia. Or if she has a little eye infection, a vet can treat it before the infection becomes much worse. A vet can also let you know whether or not your new dog has any potentially life-threatening health issues that might require more time and money than you're able to provide. It's always best to discover such problems as soon as possible so you can make the difficult decision of returning the dog if need be.

To find a vet, ask friends and family who have dogs for their recommendations. Some people even check out reviews on sites such as www.yelp.com or www.angieslist.com. If the clinic or hospital is accredited by the American Animal Hospital Association, that's a good sign that it's operating at a high level of care—though keep in mind that many outstanding practices are not accredited. Once you have a few options on the table, drop by the vets' offices to determine which one is Dr. Right. Here's what to look for:

- Make sure the facilities are clean and that the receptionist, assistants, and other employees on staff are helpful and friendly. How do they treat clients on the phone? Are they warm and welcoming to the animals that come in?

- Find out how many vets are on staff. If it's a large practice, ask if your dog will see the same doctor every time. Sometimes having multiple vets on staff is a benefit because they each have a different area of expertise. If it's a smaller practice, ask who will cover for the vet if he's on vacation or out of the office.

- Ask about office hours and how they handle emergencies. Will you have to go to another clinic if, say, your dog needs medical attention at 3 A.M.? Who will monitor your pet if she needs to stay overnight? Will the vet return phone calls directly, and if so, when? What kinds of services does she offer, and will she refer you to a specialist if need be?

- Find out about the vet's education. The vet should have received a veterinary medical degree from a school accredited by the American Veterinary Medical Association. He should also have plenty of experience, particularly with your dog's breed.

- Consider location. How far are you willing to drive for regular checkups? What about for emergencies?

- Inquire about which forms of payment the vet practice will accept. Keep in mind that most practices will not accept insurance (that is, they won't bill the insurance company on your behalf, as most human health care providers will); however, they'll help you fill out the claim so that the insurance company can reimburse you.

- Make an appointment with the vet and ask her any questions you might have about preparing for your dog's arrival. Does she seem knowledgeable? Does she communicate in a clear manner? Does she take the time to answer your questions? Are you happy with her demeanor, and do you agree with her overall philosophies about raising a dog?

- If you or your dog don't click with the vet for any reason at any point, you can always look for another one.

When You Work All Day

"My job is from 9 A.M. to 5 P.M., and I know I can't leave my dog for that long. What are my options during the workweek?"

Ideally, puppies under six months should not be left alone for more than four hours. They can't control their bladders and bowels for much longer than that. Also, dogs need exercise, and they're very social creatures—they can suffer from separation anxiety if they are left alone for too long. If you work all day and can't make it home during your lunch break, you'll have to make arrangements. Here are some options:

- **Enlist help.** Ask a trustworthy neighbor, friend, or family member to stop by your house once or twice a day to walk your dog, feed her if necessary, and give her a little love.

- **Sign up for doggy daycare.** This can be a great long-term option (though keep in mind that most places won't take puppies until they've had all their shots and until they're spayed or neutered). Doggy daycare facilities run the gamut—some are cage free, others aren't; some are indoors only, others have a yard; some are in people's homes, others are in a separate facility. When you're trying to find a daycare center, ask about hours, pricing, whether or not they separate the puppies from the bigger dogs, how many dogs they'll accept at one time, what their feeding/walking schedule is, which activities they offer, if and how they discipline dogs, and what safety procedures are in place. Also inquire about what happens in case your dog gets sick or injured.

- **Hire a dog walker.** Ask your vet or friends with dogs if they have a dog walker they'd recommend. Most importantly, choose one that comes with good reviews from other clients—always ask a potential dog walker for two or three references, and call them. When interviewing a prospect, ask how many dogs she'll walk at one time and how long she'll walk yours, if she knows basic animal first aid, and how many years of experience she has. Ask about her training methods, and make sure she uses only positive techniques when dealing with any unwanted behavior during walks, such as leash pulling. She should also be fully insured and bonded. Join her for the first walk and watch how she interacts with your dog. If you don't like what you're seeing or if she insists on using choke chains or prong collars, continue your search.

- **Have a contingency plan.** If you're in a pinch and can't arrange to have someone care for your dog while you're out of the house all day, then don't crate her. She won't be able to hold it in, and she'll wind up going potty in her sleeping area. Plus, that's way too long for a dog to be in a crate. Instead, set up a puppy-proofed, enclosed area where you can also include toys, food and water bowls, a place for your dog to sleep (which can be her crate), and even a pad for her to relieve herself on. If your dog is likely to chew up the pads, you may just need to tolerate the potty accidents in these limited instances.

Pool Fence

"My kids are finally old enough that we no longer need a pool fence. Should I leave it up for my new dog?"

A pool fence could save your dog's life. If your dog slips away from your supervision, all it takes is one minute for her to fall into the pool and drown. Puppies, who tend to be extra curious about new things and don't know any better, are among the most susceptible.

If you already have a pool fence in place, leave it up until you're certain that your dog not only can swim (some dogs, such as Bulldogs, cannot) but also knows how to get out of the pool. Even if your dog can dog paddle, if she doesn't know how to climb out, she'll eventually drown when she gets too tired.

If you don't have a fence, you can consider putting one in. However, if you don't like the idea, you can invest in a motion detector system that will set off an alarm if your dog enters the water (check the weight minimum on these devices). There's also an alarm called Safety Turtle that you put on your dog's collar—it will go off if it's submerged.

At the very least, plan on teaching your dog how to swim when she is around four months or older. Also, dedicate the necessary time to teaching her how to quickly get out of the pool in case she falls in (see page 204, chapter 9). However, always remember that when it comes to pool safety, nothing will protect your dog like your supervision. Never take your eyes off her when she's anywhere near the pool, even if she's an excellent swimmer.

Where to Put a Dog Crate

"I want to set up my dog's area before she comes home, but I'm not sure where to put her crate. What's the best spot?"

Dogs are social animals. Generally, they like being in the center of things where they can see and hear what's going on. Your dog should not be locked in a bathroom or stuck alone in the back laundry room on a regular basis. Instead, put her crate where you are frequently present, such as the family room, kitchen, or living room. Remember that crates (especially the plastic airline crates) are portable, so, for instance, you can always move yours to the home office while you're working and then to the kitchen while you're cooking dinner. At night, move the crate into your bedroom if possible—your dog will take comfort being close to you, and you'll be able to hear her whimper if she needs to go potty. If it's within your budget, consider getting more than one crate.

CHAPTER THREE

WELCOME TO THE FAMILY: STEPS FOR A SMOOTH TRANSITION

You're finally ready to bring home your new dog for the first time! You're probably elated, but you also may be a little nervous that your dog will now be completely dependent on you. You may be wondering, "How am I going to train him? What should I feed him? How do I prevent him from destroying my house? With my busy lifestyle, how can I make sure I give him enough attention?" And if you're not thinking these things, you should be. It's easy to get caught up in the excitement of having a new dog, but don't forget the responsibility that comes with it.

Don't worry, though! Whether you did your due diligence and carefully picked out the perfect dog for your family or you got a dog on a whim and feel like you may have bitten off more than you can chew, I'll get you pointed in the right direction from day one.

That's not to say that it won't take some time for you to get used to having your dog as part of your everyday routine. Likewise, it'll take your dog some time to settle in and get used to his new environment. He'll have no idea what's expected of him, which means you'll need tons of tolerance and patience right now. In other words, things will not go perfectly—and that's perfectly fine! This chapter will help make the transition as smooth as possible.

THE CAR RIDE HOME

When you pick up your dog on homecoming day, bring another person along with you so that you can focus on your pet while the driver focuses on the road. Since your dog's safety and well-being should always be first priority, the ideal way to transport a dog in a car is with a travel crate, usually made out of durable plastic. If you don't have a crate with you, then sit in the back seat with your pet and hold him on your lap or in the seat next to you. Your dog could have a potty accident or even get carsick on the way home, so protect your car and your clothes by letting him rest on an old sheet or towel.

Before the ride, walk your new dog to let him empty his bladder and tire him out a little. If you have a long journey, you'll need to stop about once an hour for potty breaks. An older dog can hold it longer, but I'd still stop hourly just to let him out of the car, since he might be anxious because of the sudden change in his environment. If your new pet is not fully vaccinated yet, avoid taking him where other dogs frequently visit, such as pet areas at highway rest stops. Instead, get off the beaten path to areas that other dogs are not likely to frequent.

Your dog may cry or whine during the car ride, but do not reprimand him in any way. Just focus on comforting him and getting him home safe and sound.

HOME SWEET HOME

When you arrive home, go *slowly*. Try to see things from your dog's perspective: a short while ago he was living in a completely different place under a different set of circumstances. Just like humans, dogs need a little time to adjust. You can let yours sniff around the front yard—ideally on a leash, if possible. However, if you have a young puppy he'll likely be very thrown off by a leash at this point, so you can let him scamper around as long as you completely control where he goes. After a few minutes, lead or carry your dog inside the house. I still remember the moment I carried my dog Venus through the front door for the first time and felt the rapid increase in her heart rate—I knew from that second on I'd always do anything I could to take care of her.

At first, simply let your dog get acclimated. Everything is new for a puppy. Even if your dog is older, this is the first time he's been in *your* house. For now, keep your dog in a contained area, such as the kitchen, cordoned off with baby gates so that he can explore. You'll want to introduce him to the rest of the house gradually over the next couple of days.

Many people are tempted to let their puppy roam freely around the house, and this can be fine for short periods of time under complete supervision. *However, the single biggest mistake that people make with a new dog is giving too much freedom way too early.* In fact, controlling your dog's environment for the first six months to one year of training is essential for best results. You must make this a priority. I'll explain how to do that throughout this chapter and the rest of the book.

MAKING INTRODUCTIONS

As far as letting your dog meet your kids or other family pets, introduce just one new variable at a time. This is not the time to invite all your relatives, friends, and neighbors over—stick with immediate family at first to maintain a calm environment. Also, take it easy; suddenly letting your dog interact with, say, the resident family cat can spell disaster in some instances. Do not rush this process. Here's how to make all family introductions go smoothly:

Introducing Children

According to the American Veterinary Medical Association, more than 4.5 million people are bitten by dogs each year, and children are not only the most likely victims but also most likely to be seriously injured.[1] That's why it's especially important to teach kids to respect a dog's space. A dog can be very thrown off by a little, fast-moving, unpredictable person, so a child should never bother a dog while he's eating or sleeping and should never rush over to a dog. Of course, that's easier said than done when dealing with kids, so it's *your* responsibility to constantly monitor all interactions between your dog and children. Part of that is helping your child make a good first impression.

First, control the situation—you don't want a dog knocking down a toddler, but you don't want a young child pulling on a puppy's tail either. Encourage your child to be gentle with the dog. Most first meetings go better when a child gives the dog a special treat such as a bit of chicken. This, at a very basic level, tells the dog, "I'm good and you can trust me." Let the child toss a piece of meat to the dog from a few feet away. *Distance is always your friend when getting your dog comfortable in a new situation.* Plus, if your dog is the type to grab treats in a rough manner, tossing the food will make things go more smoothly.

It's important to let the dog come to your child—don't let your child smother their new pet and expect the dog to just deal with it. Aim for brief, positive interactions. A good way to start might be by asking your child to sit on the ground and softly pet the dog as soon as the dog has finished the treat and seems comfortable.

Another note: Even if your child is super-excited about her new family member, please remember that this dog is *your* responsibility. Not that you shouldn't encourage your kids to play with and care for the family dog, but you need to keep your expectations realistic. Kids older than twelve can *help* train the family pet if they're serious about doing so, but it's not realistic to expect your dog to listen to kids much younger than that.

▶ Introducing Other Family Dogs

Thirty percent of people who have dogs actually have two or more in the family.[2] However, if you are bringing a second (or third!) dog home, it's important to take steps to make sure the introduction goes smoothly.

If you already have a dog, it's usually a safer bet to set up the introduction in a place neither dog identifies as his home. You might want to try somewhere in your neighborhood or a park, with both dogs on leash. I recommend using a lot of common sense and caution here.

First things first: Try to make sure both dogs are tired, since adequately exercised dogs are usually physically satisfied, less likely to react unfavorably, and generally easier to control. Start with the dogs at a distance from one another and see how they react. Whatever you do, don't force the introduction. If they ignore each other initially, that's fine; let them meet at their own pace. Then slowly let them sniff one another and check each other out. Just to be extra careful, at some point you might want to separate them for a bit to give them a breather and then try again. Dogs respond best when we ease them into new situations.

If both dogs seem very friendly and accepting of each other, bring them home and repeat these same steps outside your house at first. Then try taking it indoors. If they still look like they're doing well and there are no red flags such as nipping, or one of the dogs is trying to get away or tucking his tail between his legs, then it's okay to take the leashes off. Keep in mind that dogs might play fight, and if a younger dog is jumping all over the place, the older dog might growl a bit to tell him, "Hey, you're the new kid. Chill out." This is normal to some extent.

If you feel like your dogs are playing extremely roughly, break them up and give them a minute to relax. Think about kids and their siblings. They might start off playing and getting along, but things can quickly escalate into a squabble. This doesn't mean they can't play together; they might just need time away from each other to cool down. However, if you notice there's consistently a lot of growling, serious altercations are breaking out routinely, or one or both dogs seem particularly aggressive toward each other, limit their access to one another as much as possible (see page 157 in chapter 7 for more information on aggression).

Introducing the Family Cat

In popular culture, cats and dogs are often portrayed as mortal enemies. However, I've known plenty of dogs that live in perfect harmony with their feline counterparts. Some even become great friends. You just need to tread lightly when introducing your cat to the new family dog to avoid any problems.

When your dog is meeting your cat for the first time, remember that dogs with pent-up energy are less likely to behave well in new situations, so make sure yours has gotten enough exercise. If you have a very young puppy, it's usually easier to introduce him to a cat because, let's face it, most cats are pretty good at outsmarting puppies. For your puppy's sake, make sure your cat's claws are trimmed before any introduction. At first, keep the puppy on a leash so that he can't suddenly rush toward the cat and risk having a negative incident or getting injured. You can also put your cat in a crate (if she's fine being in one) and let the puppy sniff around. Either way, the key is to slowly allow the two animals to become comfortable with one another—a process that can take from a day or two to weeks. Using treats can help your dog create a positive association with cats. Plus, when you have good treats out, most dogs tend to be more focused on you during the introduction.

However, if you adopted an older, larger dog, especially one with lots of energy, then you have to focus more on keeping the cat safe. Definitely keep them separate at first and introduce them under very controlled circumstances over a period of days to weeks or even, in some cases, months. (Ideally, you'll give yourself a head start by choosing a dog who doesn't have a history of aggression toward other animals.) Keep your dog on a leash or have the cat behind a gate or in a crate and make sure each introduction is brief and controlled. Once you get a sense that your dog and cat are comfortable around each other—the dog isn't lunging toward the cat and barking, and the cat isn't hissing and in a crouched stance with her ears pinned back—then you can briefly take the dog off leash to see how they'll interact. Be alert: if you see anything in their body language that makes you uneasy, then intervene and take more time to get them acquainted. Remember, most people try to introduce their dog to their family cat too quickly. In a lot of cases, that just won't work.

I'd never had a cat until recently when I moved with my three Border Collies from Atlanta to New Orleans to be with my girlfriend, Bree. Bree has a cat she rescued a few years ago named Angela. Meanwhile, all of my dogs love to focus intensely on small furry animals. While I've taught them to control those impulses over the years, and they have never harmed a small animal, they still occasionally love to chase squirrels, chipmunks, and yes, cats, especially when they're on our property.

So when introducing my dogs to their new feline roommate, I knew I needed to be one step ahead of them. Move-in day came, and we made sure that Angela was in another room away from the dogs. The next day Bree held Angela in front of my dogs, one at a time, to make them aware that there was a cat in the house. We took baby steps like the ones I've explained in this section—in fact, I methodically took about two months to slowly integrate Angela into my dogs' lives. Today, I don't even think twice about leaving Angela alone with my dogs. I even catch them playing together from time to time!

If you've followed all of the advice in this section, and your dog is still apparently trying to attack your cat, see page 157 in chapter 7 to learn more about how to handle aggression. Otherwise, supervise heavily during their first interactions and be prepared to separate them if necessary. Regardless of your dog's age, make sure your cat always has a safe place by using a cat door, baby gate, or even a windowsill that only she can reach. At the very least, put her food, water, and litter box somewhere that only she can access. Also, check that the animals can't directly interact with each other when you're not around (this shouldn't be an issue if you're using a dog crate, gates, or other dog-proofed area).

Introducing the Leash

Once your dog has been home for a day or two, it's time to introduce the leash to him if you haven't done so already. If you have an older dog, chances are he's already comfortable with a leash on; but if your puppy or dog has not become accustomed to a leash, you may notice that the moment he detects any tension on it he'll temporarily panic. See things from his perspective. He has never been restrained or limited in this way before, and it must be fairly freaky for him. That's why we want to take proactive measures to encourage our dogs to accept this new device. Here's how:

1. First, let your dog smell and explore the leash for a minute—you can hold it or place it on the ground. The point is to let him know there is a new object in the room that he has to learn about. Break out the treats during this phase to help create a positive association with the leash. We want him to know that when the leash comes out, awesome stuff comes with it.

2. Next, hook the leash to your dog's harness or collar while in your living room or familiar environment and let him walk around. Don't pick up the leash or allow any tension at first. *The fewer variables we change at a time, the better.* Your dog may view the leash as a toy initially, grabbing it and running around. While we'd correct this behavior down the road, for now it's more important that the dog is in a pleasant mood.

3. After your dog has spent some time walking around with the leash dragging behind him, encourage him to come to you by making a fun sound or using a high-pitched voice. Give him a treat for his compliance. Then pick up the leash very gently for one second, still taking care to avoid tension. Drop it back on the ground and give your dog a treat as if to say, "I like that you reacted well to that first test." See what we did there? We went out of our way to start very small and greatly increase the odds of favorable behavior. This theme will be repeated in almost every instance of teaching your dog. It might seem silly to start with a tiny step like this, but if you get good at breaking things down into very small steps, your dog will learn much faster.

4. Gradually increase the time that you are holding the leash, rewarding generously along the way, which is always key when introducing new concepts. Don't be discouraged if you encounter some bucking or panic from your dog at some point. That's just your cue to slow down a bit.

5. Finally, work up to holding the leash with one hand and enthusiastically encourage your dog to follow you around the house, enticing him along the way with treats, which you can hold in your other hand. If at any point your dog has a burst of energy, resulting in tension on the leash, and he doesn't panic, celebrate and reward with an extra treat immediately. If he does panic, simply let go of the leash and encourage him to come to you and repeat the drill. It's okay if it takes a few days for your dog to accept the idea of being on a leash; most dogs just need a little time.

▶ Introducing the Crate

A dog crate can be one of your greatest dog training tools. It keeps your dog confined and safe in instances when you can't watch him, and it can also serve a huge role in housetraining and preventing destructive behaviors like chewing up your property. That's why I recommend that you introduce your dog to the crate as soon as possible.

A lot of people seem to think that crating a dog is cruel, almost like imprisoning him. And it can be if your crate is too small or your dog is spending too much time in it. However, have you ever noticed that some dogs like to sleep under tables or couches, or that they like to burrow into closets or other dark spaces? Dogs seem to like quiet, cozy nooks, and crates are no exception. If you introduce the crate in a fun way and use it appropriately, it will be not only pleasant for your pet but also a place where he seeks comfort.

So how do you get started? Putting your dog in the crate and shutting the door is *not* the way to go; that will likely just scare him and set you back a bit. Those are actually two common mistakes people make when it comes to the crate—physically putting the dog in the crate and closing the door too soon. Here's what to do instead:

1. First, throw a tasty treat into the crate and let your dog follow it willingly. Then let him come out so he sees that there's an exit option. Do this a bunch of times.

2. Next, repeat the exercise again, but this time close the door for a few seconds. Then immediately let your dog out, give him a

treat, and say something like "Yes, good dog!" Over the next few days, gradually increase the amount of time your dog spends in the crate with the door shut while you're present. (For whether or not to crate on your puppy's first night home, see below.) The slower you go during this process, the better.

3. Once your dog is spending time in the crate while you are present, then try stepping out of the room and listen to how your dog reacts when you're not there. Some whining is normal, and initially you should ignore it; however, address more extreme crying or distress by letting your dog out and taking a break from crate training. Try again later.

4. If you adopt an older dog who has a positive association with crates, then you shouldn't have a problem reacclimating him to one. However, some dogs will absolutely hate their crates, especially those who might have had negative experiences with them in the past (such as being left in them for too long, as is often the case with neglectful pet parents and puppy mill dogs). In those cases, look for an alternative such as a playpen or a puppy-proofed bathroom or laundry room.

BEDTIME

That first magical day can quickly take a turn when it's time for bed. The sweet little pup doesn't seem quite as adorable when he's waking you at 3 A.M. (Okay, fine, he's still ridiculously cute, but you could use some shut-eye!) You might get lucky and have a dog who sleeps straight through the night, but keep your expectations realistic here and don't expect a good night's sleep right away. In fact, if you have a puppy, you'll likely have to wake up once or twice to take him outside the first few weeks. Don't worry; as your dog becomes adjusted you'll both be sleeping fine. However, it can take a few weeks to get your dog on a schedule, so be patient. Most puppies will sleep through the night—about eight hours—by the time they are about twelve weeks old, some even sooner.

On that first night your dog may be scared, lonely, and out of sorts. For a puppy, it could be his first time away from his littermates and mother. Whether you plan on your dog always sleeping in your room or not, it's usually best to start him out there for the first few nights. He's going to need some comfort.

Your best bet will be to put a dog crate next to your bed. However, if your dog seems extra wary of the crate at first and you haven't gotten him used to it during the day, he probably won't be too happy in it at night. Another option is to put some old towels or blankets down next to your bed while safely securing his leash to your bed or nightstand. (Just make sure there's nothing he can chew and that he can't get tangled.) Either way, during the day give your pet age-appropriate exercise so that he is less stressed and more likely to sleep at bedtime.

If your dog cries or whines at night, try ignoring him at first. Don't pick him up right away—doing so can teach him that whining gets an immediate response of "get out of the crate and play." However, if your dog is really crying for twenty minutes or longer and you've already walked him, then it's fine to take him out and briefly reassure him. Don't do this all the time—just during those first few days when he's adjusting.

When it comes to bedtime, a lot of people lose their patience, but please don't. Having a new dog is like having a new baby in this respect. Be empathetic to what your dog has just gone through. Your job is to make him feel comfortable and safe. I promise, your dog (and you!) will sleep through the night before you know it.

SOCIALIZATION

Socialization is one of the most important things you can do for your dog, especially since it can greatly help prevent behavioral problems down the road. The socialization period, a critical time in a dog's life, occurs primarily between six and fourteen weeks. As the American Veterinary Medical Association explains, "During this time, positive experiences with other dogs, people, noises, and activities can reduce the likelihood of fearful behaviors, such as aggression and phobias, later in the dog's life."[3] Dogs who aren't properly socialized are more inclined to develop behavioral issues, which, in turn, wind up being the number one reason dogs are relinquished to shelters.[4] The key is to expose your dog to many different types of people, animals, places, sounds, and experiences, especially during those critical weeks. Continue doing so throughout your dog's entire first year. Whenever possible, bring your pet with you when you're out and about and praise him lavishly whenever he's in a new situation or around a new type of animal or person. (A few bits of meat or other treat can't hurt either!) Doing so will help teach him tolerance.

If you've adopted an older dog, don't worry—I've seen that dogs can benefit from socialization at any age. However, it can take more time and patience on your part. In some cases, if your dog has had very limited socialization and has deeply ingrained undesirable behaviors because of it, there are no quick fixes. It can take several months, even years, to see dramatic improvement on these issues, so focus on steady progress over time. However, if your dog ever shows aggressive behavior such as baring teeth or a willingness to attack, immediately remove your dog from the associated situations, animals, or people, and see page 157, chapter 7, for more information on aggression.

Overall, when exposing your dog to new animals, people, or experiences, it's crucial to create a positive association. Here's how to do that:

▶ Other Dogs

We have to teach our pets that they're not the only dogs on the block. They need to become comfortable with other dogs of all shapes and sizes so that they are not fearful, aggressive, or both when they encounter them throughout their lives. Many people make the false assumption that, because their dog gets along with the neighbor's dog and the other dogs in the family, this is sufficient socialization. Consider this from a human perspective: you may get along with your best friend, siblings, and parents, but that does not mean you're going to get along with all other people. You've got to work on that. Think about it—if those were the only people you hung out with, you'd probably act *very* differently when you encountered strangers.

It's crucial to focus on socializing your dog with other dogs who you *know* are friendly. The last thing you want is for your dog to encounter another dog who lunges at him or tries to bite him. So if you meet a person with a dog you'd like yours to meet, ask how that dog interacts with others. If the person is hesitant or says anything other than, "He loves other dogs!" politely move on. Rule out potentially bad experiences as often as you can. There are plenty of other dogs for yours to interact with.

This is not the time to take your dog to a dog park and let him run free. For one, he can easily encounter a not-so-friendly dog and wind up having a negative experience. This is extremely common at dog parks. Also, if your dog is a puppy, you need to make sure he's around only healthy dogs who are vaccinated so he doesn't catch a serious illness.

During introductions to other dogs, follow the same guidelines I outlined earlier in this chapter for when you introduce your new pet to the resident family dog. Watch for body language: if the dogs are sniffing each other and wagging their tails, then there's a good chance they want to play. Also, if one or both dogs does the "play bow"—crouching down on their front legs, butt up in the air (a universal dog invitation to play)—that's usually a sure sign that things are going well. However, if you notice any excessive growling, snapping, or if either dog has his tail between his legs and seems fearful or aggressive in any way, find another dog for yours to socialize with.

▶ People

It's important to expose your dog to people of various ages, sizes, and races, as well as to people who look different in any way (ranging from a person in uniform, such as a mailman, to a person with a mustache or one who uses a walker or a wheelchair). At a distance, so as not to alarm your dog, try putting on a big hat and sunglasses and popping open your umbrella—these are all things that he might find disturbing if he's not accustomed to them. Definitely don't forget to let your dog meet plenty of men—dogs sometimes find men intimidating due to their large statures and deep voices. Recently I worked with a dog named Milli (short for millimeter), a rescue who was found as a stray on the roadside. Whenever she met a new man, she became fearful, barked incessantly, and wouldn't go near him. While Milli may have had a bad experience with men in the past, the most likely explanation of her behavior was a simple lack of socialization with men. So my goal at that first training session was to communicate to her that she could trust me. After a few hours with her, she went from being standoffish and completely wary of me to letting me pet her and even play with her. Of course, that successful session didn't mean that Milli would now be okay with all men or even with me on future visits—it can take weeks to many months for a dog to generalize like that. However, it was a start.

Help ensure that your pet will have a positive experience by picking people who will handle him gently. You should be particularly cautious around children, who can be unintentionally rough. Whenever you are socializing your dog, bring good treats with you and encourage other people to give them to your dog. Assuming your dog is reacting well, ask others to softly pet him, preferably under the chin, not on top of the head. This helps communicate to him that people should not be met with fear.

▶ Life Experiences

Along with socializing your dog with other animals and with people, it's important to make him comfortable in various scenarios, ranging from driving in the car and hearing sirens to encountering a hairdryer, staircases, a vacuum cleaner, or even popcorn popping in the microwave. Let him see people riding bikes, construction workers, and lawn mowers. The more experiences, sights, and sounds, the better.

The key is to go slowly and to break down such new experiences into little steps, especially if your dog seems reluctant. For instance, with a vacuum cleaner, first let your dog sniff it (while it's off, of course!) Then turn it on for one second, just to show your dog that it makes noise. If all goes well, gradually increase the time you keep the vacuum on and take a step back if your dog ever seems frightened at all. Give your dog a treat and praise every step of the way.

ASK *Zak*

Adjusting to a New Home

"My puppy just came home a few days ago, and he seems a little droopy. Is it possible he's stressed out or sad from leaving his mother and littermates?"

Put yourself in your dog's place. He's in a completely new environment, no longer with his mother and littermates, and surrounded by humans he doesn't know. Of course he might be a little out of sorts! It is extremely common for a new dog (regardless of age) to be more mellow or subdued at first and then to start to come out of his shell a bit over the first few days. However, if after some time your dog still hasn't seemed to adjust, take him to the vet to make sure there's no underlying medical condition that's contributing to his behavior.

Sleeping in Your Bed

"Is it okay to let my dog sleep in my bed with me?"

This is a very personal decision. Some people never want their dogs in their beds; others wouldn't have it any other way. There's no right or wrong answer; it's up to you.

If you've just brought your dog home, I'd wait until he's older and has some training under his belt before letting him up on the bed. Cleaning an accident off the floor is one thing, but getting the stains and smells off a comforter or mattress is a lot more difficult. However, once your dog is a little older and housetrained, if you want to allow him on the bed, go for it. (You may have heard that letting your dog do that will make him view you as an equal and it'll be difficult to train him. That's a myth—there's absolutely no science to back up that idea.) Just a few things to keep in mind: If you have allergies, experts recommend keeping your dog out of your bed to keep symptoms at bay. Also, there's the chance you might not get as much shut-eye. According to a survey by the Mayo Clinic Sleep Disorders Center, 53 percent of people reported that their sleep was disrupted somewhat by their pet every night.[5]

On the flip side, there's a reason so many people sleep with their dogs: they provide comfort, protection, and warmth. I love it when my dogs sleep in bed with me. Sure, I don't have as much room, and I have to change my sheets every few days because the dogs shed. To me, it's totally worth it for that extra together time.

Feeding Your Dog

"At what point can I switch my dog's food from what he was eating at the breeder's?"

If possible, wait a few days or weeks before switching to a new food—your dog has enough changes to deal with right now! However, once you're ready to make the switch, then do so gradually to avoid stomach problems such as diarrhea. For three days, fill one-quarter of the bowl with the new food and three-quarters with the old. Then, for the next three days, the bowl should be split half with the new food, half with the old. Lastly, spend a few days serving three-quarters of the new food and one-quarter of the old. In terms of *what* to feed your dog, see chapter 8 for a guide to your options.

Time to See the Vet

"I just brought my dog home. Can I give him a few weeks to settle in before rushing him off to a medical visit?"

Actually, I'd schedule a vet visit within the first forty-eight hours of bringing him home. First of all, the vet will check for any health problems and will make sure your dog is up to date on his deworming and vaccinations. She will also help answer questions about basic care for your new family member.

Taking your new dog on a trip to the vet is also a vital part of socialization—vet visits are going to be a part of his life, so you want that first one to be as pleasant as possible. One way you can help is by getting your dog used to human touch from day one. Pretend to examine your dog: gently and carefully massage his paws, rub his belly, lift his tail, touch his ears and even his gums, so that when the vet does these things your dog is already used to it. You might also bring along some treats on the first few visits. Also, make sure that your dog has gotten exercise before the visit so that he's burned off some energy and is more likely to handle the new situation well. Of course, it's important to choose the right vet (see page 45, chapter 2).

Socialization and Vaccinations

"I know I'm supposed to start socializing my puppy, but how do I do that if he hasn't had all his vaccinations yet?"

As I've explained, socialization is crucial for dogs, especially young puppies. However, your dog won't receive his last vaccination dose until sixteen weeks, and many experts advise against letting puppies near other dogs because of the risk of various contagious illnesses. For that reason, you'll need to avoid other dogs unless you know they've been vaccinated.

So what should you do? The good news is that you will find plenty of dogs you *can* socialize with. Ask friends, family, or neighbors who have vaccinated dog-friendly dogs if you can come over for a play date. And one of the best ways to socialize a new puppy is by enrolling in a puppy class. There's some controversy about this—while some experts say that no dogs under the age of sixteen weeks should attend puppy classes because they haven't been fully vaccinated, many others say it's far more important that the dog is socialized. The American Veterinary Society of Animal Behavior says dogs as young as seven to eight weeks can start puppy classes as long as they have their first set of shots at least one week before the class starts and a first deworming; people should also keep their pets up to date with vaccines throughout the class.[6] Also, a study in the *Journal of the American Animal Hospital Association* found that puppies who had at least one set of shots but weren't yet fully vaccinated were at no greater risk of a parvovirus infection (a highly contagious viral illness common among dogs) after attending socialization classes than vaccinated puppies who didn't attend those classes.[7] That said, most dog trainers should require proof of vaccinations before allowing puppies to attend their classes.

First Bath

"I just picked my ten-week-old puppy up from the shelter and he's filthy. Is he too young to be bathed?"

You probably want to smother your new dog with kisses—but not if he's covered in urine and feces! In general, most dogs won't need baths until they are three months old or older, but if yours is dirty you can certainly bathe him. However, it's important to know how to do it right. Check out page 173, chapter 8, for a complete section on grooming and bathing your dog. Also, don't get into the habit of bathing your dog too often, as doing so can strip natural oils from his fur and skin.

Holding a Dog

"My young son loves picking up our new pet, but I want to make sure he does it correctly. What should I tell him?"

It's very important that you and everyone else in your household learn how to pick up your dog properly. Place one hand or arm under his chest and use your other hand or arm to support his hind legs and backside. Never try to carry him by his paws or by the scruff of his neck. This can be unpleasant or even painful and can make your dog fear being held.

Fearfulness

"I've been socializing my puppy, but he still seems afraid of every noise, every person, and every dog he encounters. Is this normal? And what should I do?"

Yes, this is normal for puppies. Puppies are taking in a massive amount of new information, and there are going to be many things that don't make sense to them. Address these situations much as you would with a toddler, with lots of patience and understanding. When you expose your dog to a new animal, person, or situation, if he seems hesitant at first, back away from the situation, give him a second to adjust, and try again when he settles down. However, if he seems really nervous or frightened, don't insist that he just deal with it. Instead, save that socialization lesson for another time. Remember, baby steps work best in these situations.

If your dog is still fearful as he gets older, you can help him to some extent but expect small amounts of progress at a time. First, identify when your dog is likely to become fearful. Preempt these moments by doing what you can to distract your dog and get him into a happy mood. For example, if you know a garbage truck is approaching outside and your dog is likely to be distressed by the noise, try getting him to play with you by enticing him with his favorite toy before the truck even gets in front of your house. If your dog is scared of thunderstorms, the key is to intercede before the thunder occurs: use the lightning flash as a cue that it's time to distract your dog with, say, a game of tug-of-war or a good treat. If your dog's anxiety is very high, you may need to reassure him by petting him softly. Act normal and understanding, but don't behave in a frantic way that your dog could potentially interpret as uncertainty. Just be cool.

In the case of being fearful of people, encourage strangers to give your dog good treats or, if he is uncomfortable with being approached, to toss them near your dog. The treats get your dog's mind off of what's making him nervous and onto something he likes. This is how you begin to gain momentum.

Finally, know that not every issue is 100 percent curable. Some dogs may remain timid in certain situations for the rest of their lives. Remember, dogs are living beings, and it's perfectly normal for them to sometimes feel afraid just as we do. Although my dog Venus is not as afraid of thunderstorms as she used to be, she's still pretty scared—just as I've never gotten over my own fear of heights. However, if your dog seems excessively fearful, talk to your vet about other strategies or interventions that might help. Also, if your dog's fear seems to manifest as growling, snapping, or other forms of aggression, see page 157, chapter 7, to learn more about how to handle this serious situation.

CHAPTER FOUR

DOG TRAINING REVOLUTION: THE KEY PRINCIPLES

I've been a dog trainer for more than twelve years now, and in that time I've had the honor of working directly with thousands of dogs and reaching millions of people through YouTube and television. I have the greatest job in the world, and I wouldn't trade it for anything.

However, during these years I've seen a lot of things in my industry that fly in the face of common sense and ethics. Even though many studies have shown that dogs learn better through positive reinforcement training than through force and intimidation, far too many traditional trainers either don't know this or are unwilling to accept it. Many of them talk about the importance of being the "alpha." They advise people with dogs to yank and pop leashes, knee their dogs in the chest to stop them from jumping, and flip them onto their backs to show them who's boss. Most use devices such as metal choke chains and electric or prong collars. They tell people that their dogs might try to take over their lives due to underlying control issues, even though there's no real evidence to back that up.

Such ideas of being "dominant" or the "pack leader" have become so popular and ingrained in the dog training world that I've become motivated to speak out against these old-fashioned beliefs. Many people trust the "professionals" who perpetuate these ideas, and they follow their advice, thinking they are doing right by their dogs. Instead, they are actually teaching their pets to behave just to avoid discomfort and pain, not because they have learned to communicate effectively with them. I'll show you what's possible when you focus on establishing a loving relationship with your dog rather than relying on the same old misinformation that's been around for ages.

My goal is clear and simple: to continue helping to disrupt the dog training industry and to steer it toward more ethical practices while inspiring a new generation of people to connect with their dogs in a way they've never been taught before. There are very effective, humane ways of training dogs, completely backed by science, and I'm going to share them with you throughout this book. I am passionate about doing anything I can to help encourage progress in the way we teach our dogs.

The next two chapters will focus on specific how-tos of training such as housetraining, walking on a leash, and "sit" and "stay"; this one will give you all the fundamentals you need no matter what you're teaching your dog. I'll explain the guiding principles of my training methods so that you, too, can become part of the Dog Training Revolution!

EIGHT COMMON MYTHS IN DOG TRAINING

Before I delve into the training methods that really work, first I'll shed some light on commonly held misconceptions about dogs to make sure we're starting off on the same page:

Myth #1: Dogs are domesticated wolves, so you need to establish yourself as pack leader.
Truth: Have you ever heard that the surefire way to be a good dog trainer is to be the "alpha"? I did, years before I became a dog trainer, and even

I thought it sounded reasonable at the time: dogs descended from wolves, and wolves supposedly live in hierarchal packs, so it made sense.

Actually, there's little to no truth behind this idea. No one is arguing that dogs aren't *descendants* of ancient wolves—they certainly are. However, dogs are not wolves, but unique animals predisposed to learn very advanced concepts from human beings. We likely first selectively bred today's domestic dogs at least fifteen thousand years ago to cohabitate with us, provide companionship, and perform certain tasks such as hunting, herding, or alerting us when a stranger is near. To ignore the human influence in the domestic dog reflects a failure to acknowledge why the modern dog even exists at all. Yet many mainstream dog trainers seem to completely disregard this central point in favor of using methods that undermine the intelligence of our dogs.

Also, these trainers are basing their philosophy on an archaic understanding of wolf behavior that has been discredited by researchers who study wolves extensively.[1] In the 1940s, animal behaviorist Rudolph Schenkel found that when wolves are forced into captivity, they fight for top status or what he referred to as the "alpha." For decades, this concept reigned in the dog training world, and one of the world's leading wolf experts, L. David Mech, discussed it extensively in his popular 1970 book. However, thirty years later Mech himself completely refuted the "alpha" wolf concept, so much so that he has pleaded with his publisher to stop printing that previous book.[2] He had found, through his own extensive research, that the dog training industry was basing their teachings on a highly artificial situation. Yes, when wolves are randomly placed in confinement together, they do fight for resources; however, that happens only when these animals are in a very unnatural environment. "Wolves in the wild—the wolves that our dogs descended from—get to the top of their pack merely by maturing, mating, and producing offspring," says Mech. "In fact, leadership roles are simply parental roles. The pack is actually a family social structure, a lot like human families."

It baffles me that many mainstream trainers are still promoting ideas that have long been rejected by the very experts who study this topic most. Any training ideology that relies on your being a "pack leader" or an "alpha" instead of a loving parent to your dog is fundamentally flawed from day one.

Myth #2: Domination is the only way to get a dog to listen to you.

Truth: Real teaching is about communication, not domination. Our goal when teaching a dog should be not to make a dog do something by forcing her into submission, but to make a dog *want* to do something. Trying to dominate your dog by yelling at her, flipping her on her back in an "alpha roll," or using certain collars designed to create discomfort or pain will only greatly hinder both your relationship with your pet and the training process.

I know this can be confusing because many well-known trainers promote such dominant techniques. However, what we are really communicating to a dog when we rely on these tools is: "If you do something I don't like—even if it's something that comes naturally to you, like walking fast or chasing a squirrel—I'm going to make you uncomfortable." Such training focuses on teaching what a dog *shouldn't* do rather than what she *should* do.

Can these methods be effective? If your definition of "effective" is getting mediocre results, then yes, to some extent they can be. I suppose if I thought I'd experience something unpleasant every time I walked a bit too fast, I'd obey too. But there's a price to pay for this: your training will not be as effective and enjoyable as it could be for both you and your dog, and such tactics could even undermine your dog's trust. Furthermore, your dog will not behave consistently when you take those special collars off or don't use forceful methods. When you rely on an external device to get what you want, it's simply a crude patch designed to combat the unwanted behavior rather than to emphasize good behavior. And when that patch isn't there, dogs know the difference and often go right back to the unwanted behavior. It's as though they think, "Oh, I'm not wearing that unpleasant collar now, so I can do whatever I want."

Some people might argue that while positive training is okay for some breeds, other breeds *need* forceful, punishment-based training because they are aggressive, powerful dogs. Let me respond to that. First, while some dogs may be more challenging or have aggression issues, that's definitely not specific to breed. As I explained in chapter 1, the whole idea that certain breeds such as Pit Bulls have violent tendencies is completely false—when you hear stories of such dogs attacking other animals or people, it's usually because either they have been trained to do so by a human or they have more serious underlying issues. Of course, if you have a larger dog, it's particularly important to make sure she doesn't lunge on the leash or jump up on people simply because she can cause more harm than, say, a Yorkie, due to her size. But that applies to *any* larger dog—from a German Shepherd to a Goldendoodle—and has absolutely nothing to do with breed.

Positive training works with virtually any dog. In fact, if you *do* have a dog with aggression issues, studies have shown that using forceful methods will likely make the behaviors worse. For instance, one study in the *Journal of Applied Animal Behavior* found that confrontational methods such as striking dogs, intimidating them, alpha rolls, and staring them down often led to an aggressive response.[3] "In almost all cases, dogs are aggressive because they are afraid and feel threatened in some way," explains Meghan Herron, DVM, DACVB, lead author of the study and director of the Behavioral Medicine Clinic at The Ohio State University College of Veterinary Medicine. "When you use confrontational methods, you are just making yourself more threatening and increasing your dog's motivation to use aggression against you. It's like fighting fire with fire." What about the dogs who do seem to reduce their aggressive behaviors in the face of these methods? "Sometimes people can scare their dogs enough that the animals achieve a state of learned helplessness—they just sit and take it, even though they're exhibiting signs of panic such as an increased heart rate and panting," Dr. Herron explains. "Some of these dogs eventually lose this inhibition and their aggression comes back much worse than before, as though they've snapped. And for those who don't, they remain shut down and often live in a state of perpetual fear." I'd hope that anyone who thinks this is acceptable would strongly reconsider the way they approach teaching dogs.

Myth #3: Only puppies can learn new things.

Truth: Apparently this line of thinking has been around a loooong time: In 1534, an Englishman named John Fitzherbert wrote in *The Boke of Husbandry,* "The dogge must lerne it, when he is a whelpe, or els it will not be: for it is harde to make an olde dogge to stoupe."[4] Today's translation: "You can't teach an old dog new tricks."

I know that clichés often have a good bit of truth to them, but that's definitely not the case with this one. I have worked with thousands of dogs, and I can attest that you can most certainly teach dogs of all ages just about anything. More than half the dogs I've worked with in my career were adult dogs, not puppies. I even had a dog in one of my basic training classes who was fourteen years old—he did wonderfully and passed with flying colors. And to this day, I enjoy teaching new concepts to my own dogs, who are all in double digits now. In fact, I recently taught Alpha Centauri to run outside, pick up a package from my front yard, and bring it back into the house. He doesn't mind the rain like I do!

Bottom line: Dogs simply love to learn at all ages, and you should always continue teaching them new tricks and concepts to keep them mentally stimulated. No offense to Mr. Fitzherbert, but don't buy into this old idea for a second!

Myth #4: Positive training means never disciplining your dog.

Truth: Just because you're not forcing your dog into submission doesn't mean you're going to let her walk all over you. Positive training does include consequences for unwanted behaviors, but it's very different from the aggressive methods of traditional trainers.

I have no problem with communicating that you do not like something your dog does. If you catch your dog getting into the garbage, telling her "No, don't do that" in a calm tone and then removing access to the trash is very logical to me. Or, in the case of jumping on guests, removal from the environment for a few minutes in a good ol' time-out can be very effective, too. The problem comes when you start saying "No!" a lot more often than you say "Yes." If this is the case, then you are *reacting* to your dog's actions rather than taking the appropriate initiative to teach her how you'd like her to behave. The goal is to show your dog the behaviors you do like so the emphasis is more on the positive. So after you remove the garbage and get your dog to sit and focus her attention on you, then reward the positive behavior. Follow through and go that extra mile! When you learn to snap into training mode and follow through like this, you'll start to see a dramatic acceleration in your results.

Do I physically correct a dog from time to time? You bet I do, but only in rare circumstances. Here are the criteria I apply when putting my hands on a dog or forcing her to do something: Would I correct a three-year-old child in the manner I'm about to correct this dog? If not, then I don't do it. Here's an example: Let's suppose I'm standing on a street corner with my dog on leash sitting next to me. Suddenly, there's a distraction across the street and my dog attempts to run into the street toward it. I certainly will restrain my dog and walk away from the distraction abruptly, in the same way that I would grab a child's hand and pull her away from something that put her in harm's way. By definition, this is a physical correction. However, I limit physical corrections to when I'm preventing my dog from potentially being injured or causing harm to another being. Keep in mind, however, that a correction like the one I just described is a far cry from a restrictive, aggressive pop with a metal collar around a dog's throat. There's really no comparison.

Lastly, keep in mind that even the physical correction I just described is not ideal. As you'll learn throughout this book, when you effectively prepare your dog for certain situations, then for the most part *no* physical correction will ever be necessary.

▶ Myth #5: Once you use treats, your dog will never listen without them.

Truth: You can definitely wean off treats. However, people often expect that once their dog has demonstrated she understands a particular concept or trick with a treat, she should immediately start doing it without one all the time. That usually doesn't work. If your dog refuses to do something without a treat, this likely means you have attempted to cut treats out of the equation too early and your dog doesn't get it yet.

Your dog will certainly learn to listen without treats, but you'll probably need to use them longer than you intuitively might think, possibly up to six months after she first learns a behavior. However,

I'm talking about your dog knowing a skill completely. For her to do that, she'll need a lot of repetition and have to practice under various circumstances. For instance, say your dog sits for you when you are home alone even if you don't give her a treat; however, when you take her to a park where there are lots of distractions, she doesn't. That's because dogs don't generalize well. In fact, *the single biggest thing you can do to throw your dog off is to change her environment or other variables.* When you do, you'll need to reteach her that skill or trick in the new environment. Using a lot of treats or other rewards with sincere encouragement simply motivates your dog to do the behavior under a variety of circumstances those first several months, which is more important than insisting she does it without a treat right away.

Also, once you think your dog knows a skill completely, don't just cut out the treats cold turkey. Instead, I recommend following the principle of intermittent reinforcement. You might notice that after first teaching your dog something new, a time when you should reward heavily, that you might be able to get a "free one" without treating. That's because you are keeping your dog guessing—dogs really excel when you randomly reward, and the goal is to make sure yours can't decipher a pattern—so you avoid a pattern by mixing it up. Perhaps give a treat for a particular behavior, then skip the treat the next two times your dog does it, and then treat three times in a row.

People may argue that using treats is bribery, but I promise you it's not. Remember, one of the most important elements of my training program is learning how to communicate with your dog, and treats will help you do just that. They are a catalyst that helps keep your pet's attention on you and encourages her by letting her know she's on the right track. On top of that, researchers who have studied dogs' brains found that while food does motivate dogs, they are also greatly influenced by social interactions with humans.[5] I couldn't agree more! While you still need the treats at first to ingrain the particular behavior you're looking for, combining that with lots of love and genuine sincerity will only encourage your dog further. So my goal isn't to get my dogs to sit when I ask them only because they might get a treat. I want them sitting because they are listening to me, respecting me, enjoying my attention, and trusting that I have their best interests at heart.

▶ Myth #6: Behaviors such as jumping indicate that your dog is trying to control you.

Truth: This one really gets me! Your dog is not attempting to initiate a coup when she jumps on you after you return from work. Look at her body language. Her ears are probably pinned back, her tail is wagging, and if she could talk, she'd probably say, "I missed you so much! Let's go do stuff together!" I call this enthusiasm and joy, and I'm not really sure how this is so commonly confused with dog-to-human dominance.

When dogs exhibit behaviors such as tugging on the leash or jumping on guests, it's not because they are trying to assert dominance as part of their overall strategy aimed at achieving a higher status in the family. Also, doing things such as letting your dog through the doorway first, allowing her on your bed, and feeding her before you eat is *certainly* not going to make her think she's now in control. These are ideas based purely on myths.

So what are behaviors such as excessive jumping or leash lunging really all about? I know that when dogs act out it almost always has to do with a lack of the kind of exercise that engages both the mind and body, like fetch or other dog sports. Here's an example: I once worked with a dog named Lafitte, a very energetic dog who had the unusual habit of, well, lunging at and attacking full-size trees. Lafitte is no small dog, either, and when he did this it was a sight to see. I know that many trainers would simply say that Lafitte is a dominant dog, slap a choke chain on him, and yank away until he was defeated and exhausted. However, I figured Lafitte was a dog with a lot of pent-up energy who didn't have a regular outlet to release it. While his primary person, Rachel, certainly tried, it was hard to keep up with his demanding needs all of the time.

Lafitte didn't care about achieving dominance; he just wanted to do something, anything! Even if it meant that the best way to release some energy was to use the closest tree as a toy. Sure enough, after spending some time with him, in a single training session I was able to teach Lafitte the concept of not attacking trees. Rachel also started playing with him on a more regular basis and has reported that his behavior has improved greatly. I elaborate on the specific issue of leash pulling on page 147, chapter 7, but the bigger point here is that I taught Lafitte without trying to dominate him or cause him discomfort. I simply took the time to first understand why he was behaving in a certain way and then took steps to preempt that behavior by communicating in a way that encouraged him to listen to me.

Myth #7: Dogs can't understand that much, so speak in very simple terms.

Truth: This is one of my biggest pet peeves. Most trainers advise you to keep your phrasing very simple and limit your requests to one word at a time. They say that dogs can't understand all that much, so the fewer words you use with your dog, the better. There's certainly validity to this when *introducing* a brand-new concept like "sit," but there's nothing wrong with evolving your language after the first few weeks of basic training. Saying "Sit down please," "Have a seat," or whatever else you want to say to your dog can actually help broaden her vocabulary. Personally, I love being able to interact with my dogs by using everyday speech.

Several studies have clearly shown that dogs can have a huge vocabulary, comparable to a toddler's. Stanley Coren, PhD, a leading expert in canine intelligence and author of *How to Speak Dog: Mastering the Art of Human-Dog Communication*, among other titles, has found that the average dog can learn at least 165 words. Highly intelligent dogs can learn 250 words, or even considerably more. One Border Collie named Chaser holds the current known record, at more than one thousand words, and she most certainly understands some sentences and grammatical semantics.[6] I know she's an outlier, but her story shows that dogs are a lot more capable than most people think they are.

I can verify that dogs can understand simple sentences, provided you speak this way often. That's not to say that you shouldn't use one-word requests such as "sit" and "stay." But you don't have to always limit your phrases to one word at a time. You also don't have to worry that you are going to confuse your dog—they understand slight nuances in language and context just as we do. My own dogs very clearly know the difference between "let go" and "let's go." Also, years ago when I used to perform with my dogs in stunt dog shows, I would say "Down please" to tell them to get off a platform they were standing on. This did not confuse them when I'd later ask them to lie down by saying, yet again, "Down please."

There's also no need to dumb down your grammar. If your dog is barking, for instance, you can abandon phrases such as "No bark!" Instead, use proper grammar by saying "Stop barking please," and teach your dog your language as you would teach a young child. Feel free to speak in a way that comes naturally. You'll be shocked by what your dog can understand.

Myth #8: You can teach your dog only one thing at a time.
Truth: Dogs are remarkably intelligent and capable of "walking and chewing gum at the same time." Just like humans, your dog can process many concepts simultaneously. Of course, I'm not saying to go crazy here and expect your dog to master ten tricks or skills in one day. There's a fine line between covering multiple concepts and confusing your dog. You'll have to find that line with your own dog, but a general rule of thumb is between two and four simple tasks at a time.

As for me, I like to introduce the concepts of "sit," "down," "up," and "stand" in the same training session with most dogs (see page 125, chapter 6, to learn how to teach this). That's four things! You are not only encouraging your dog to multitask mentally, which is great exercise for her brain, but also planting the seeds for more intermediate or advanced skills down the road that require more than one step.

Most importantly, don't think you have to completely perfect a concept before moving on to the next one. Many people assume they need to, say, master housetraining before they move on to basic training, as though it's sequential. Again, I want to make sure that this is *not* your mind-set. While you're housetraining your dog, you should work on other basic skills. Dogs want to work with humans, and by encouraging your dog to learn lots of things, you're only speeding up her success.

KEY TRAINING PRINCIPLES

Now that you know which myths are either preventing or slowing progress when it comes to teaching our dogs, let's go over the fundamentals that truly work.

Put simply, if an outcome to a behavior is positive, then the dog is likely to repeat that behavior, and if the outcome is not favorable, then that dog is less likely to repeat it. This is generally true for virtually all animals, including people. Unfortunately, the dog training world is full of people who place entirely too much emphasis on the latter part of that statement. However, *training is far more effective when you focus on emphasizing what you like more than what you don't like.*

Think about your favorite teacher when you were in school. Let's say you asked her for help with a particular concept or problem. What did she do? Did she yell at you? Did she blame you for not paying attention? Did she slap you on the wrist? No. She probably said something like, "Sit down and let's go over it again. I'll help you understand it better." She may have even acknowledged that the concept is hard, and that it was okay if you didn't get it instantly. She probably patiently explained things slowly and clearly, and her mood was light. Her goal was simply to make sure she was communicating the lesson effectively to you.

Now think about a teacher you *didn't* like. Maybe that teacher was annoyed when you asked for clarification. Possibly he blamed you and pointed out all the things you were doing wrong, rather than trying to help you reason through the problem. He might have discouraged you, and you may have even feared him. You probably know what I'm talking about; many of us have unfortunately had at least one teacher like that.

Compare these two encounters—one teacher probably made you excited about learning and the other made you dread it. Both approaches may have gotten results, but which do you think was more effective for the long term? Certainly the kind teacher's. We can apply these same ideologies to the dog training world. By using positive methods, you will become an understanding, engaging teacher, and your dog will love learning from you!

Here are the six most important tenets to my training program that you need to know to become that favorite teacher:

Training Principle #1: Bonding with Your Dog

From the moment you bring your dog home, one of your main focuses should be your bond with her. That's because having an exceptionally well-behaved dog is primarily a by-product of having a relationship based on love, respect, and understanding.

The good news is that it's easy to bond with dogs—they are hardwired to want to connect with us, so much so that researchers have found that dogs would rather spend time with humans than with their own kennelmates![7] As much as we love dogs, it turns out they think we're pretty awesome, too. Studies have shown that during human-animal interaction, levels of oxytocin (the "bonding" hormone) increase for both the person *and* the dog.[8] Also, Gregory Berns, MD, PhD, a neuroscientist at Emory University and author of *How Dogs Love Us*, spent years studying the canine brain by using MRI technology. By looking at brain activity, he found that dogs and humans experience emotions in a similar way.

So how do you bond with your dog? Have fun! The fastest way to achieve a bond with most dogs is through activities that involve play, such as fetch, tug-of-war, or even a game of chase in the backyard. As Plato once said, "You can discover more about a person in an hour of play than in a year of conversation." That certainly applies to dogs, too.

Bonding is also a matter of letting your dog know that she can trust you and depend on you. That means keeping her water bowl filled, feeding and walking her at expected intervals, and speaking to her in a kind voice. You'll find that dogs are pretty easy to bond with when you meet their basic needs and wants.

My students become the best teachers to their dogs when they tap into the part of their brain that helps them be good parents. Don't have kids? Me neither, but I think that most of us have it within us to learn how to "parent" someone else. You might think, "Well, parenting a child and parenting a dog are very different things." True, but there are more similarities than you may realize. One study found that, just as with children, dogs are more likely to interact in an environment where they might otherwise feel apprehensive when they have a "secure base"—a person they feel confident and secure around.[9] Just as a child might not walk into a birthday party at someone else's house without his mother or father right by his side, a hesitant dog might feel more secure in a new situation because you're next to her. With that reassurance, she may relax enough to explore and play. This isn't anthropomorphizing dogs; this is science.

Training Principle #2: The Importance of Exercise

Like humans, dogs need to keep physically active to stay healthy. However, it's about much more than just their health. From a teaching perspective, you shouldn't expect a moderate- to high-energy dog to absorb new concepts and focus on the lesson at hand until she has exercised and used up some of her energy. Also, if your dog has an unwanted behavior—say, she likes to shred apart your furniture every time you leave the house, incessantly jump on guests who come to your door, or dig up the backyard—the source is likely a lack of regular mental and physical exercise. Exercise isn't optional for many dogs; it's a necessity.

Until around the start of the twentieth century, dogs had appropriate outlets for all that energy—many actually had jobs and performed certain roles such as hunting or herding. Yes, our culture has changed dramatically, and dogs are rarely required to do many of the things they were initially bred to do. That doesn't mean we shouldn't continue to challenge them. For example, my three Border Collies were specifically bred to herd sheep, and while not all Border Collies necessarily have the drive and energy for this kind of activity, mine certainly do. Now I'll confess, I don't have any sheep in my yard in New Orleans, but I do have Frisbees and balls, so I'm able to give my dogs an outlet: to work with a person to perform a physical goal. So while they don't herd sheep, they'll chase a ball and bring it back, and this appears to give them great contentment. Dogs, at their core, require regular interaction with people—and when you couple such interaction with exercise, you can expect better results in training.

For low- to medium-energy dogs, walks, a trip to a dog park, and letting them run around the yard may do the trick. However, for those level three dogs who have tons of energy and are always raring to go, those activities aren't going to cut it. So what will? As I mentioned earlier, playing fetch is the most efficient way to satisfy a dog both mentally and physically.

Fetch

Here's what you need to know to teach fetch:

1. First, let's make sure we're talking about the same thing when it comes to fetch. I define the game as follows: you throw a toy; your dog chases it, picks it up, brings it back, and lets it go readily. Your dog is chasing a moving object; this should not be confused with "retrieve"—your dog picking up a still object off in the distance. It can take a good two to twelve weeks for your dog to learn a polished, fluid game of fetch, so don't get frustrated if yours doesn't learn it immediately. Give her some time.

2. Don't use treats. Trying to teach a dog to fetch within minutes of using food is a bad idea in most cases, as the dog is in food mode and less likely to be "grabby" with her mouth. The reward for a proper fetch should be the toy or object you're playing with, not something edible.

3. Make sure your dog *loves* the toy you're playing fetch with. That might take a bit of trial and error. When I first got my dog Supernova, he had little interest in playing fetch with the Frisbee. One day I was at a pet supply store with him and noticed he was fascinated with a cat toy that looked like a feather duster. Instead of thinking, "That's not a dog toy. Let's keep going!" I bought the toy, ripped off the feathers, and taped them to the Frisbee. That was all it took: Supernova has loved playing fetch with the Frisbee ever since and even performed in many Frisbee shows before hundreds of thousands of people in his career. Experiment with a variety of toys (I recommend trying a rope toy at first) and, if necessary, think outside of the box.

4. Don't just throw the item and expect your dog to run after it. First, you have to get her really interested in it. Try playing keep-away with the item or pretend you are playing with the toy yourself and having *a lot* of fun. The idea is to entice your dog to grab it.

5. Play tug-of-war with the item. *This is a critical step of teaching fetch.* Once your dog starts playing tug-of-war with an object,

that's a really good sign that she not only loves the object but is also well on her way to learning fetch.

6. Teach "let go." If the key to teaching a dog to like a toy is to make it exciting, then the key to teaching her to let go of the item is to make it uninteresting. Keep the toy in your hand but make sure it's absolutely still, as though it's in a vise. Also, act bored and dull, as though you couldn't care less that your dog is pulling on the toy. Don't look at her, and certainly don't move the toy in any way. This may take a few seconds or minutes. Be patient. Eventually, your dog will become bored with the toy and let go of it; the *split second* she does, tell her "Yes!" and give the toy back to her as a reward for proper behavior. (Most people wait too long to reward with the toy at first during these critical successes. Do your best not to make that mistake.) This tells her, "I have no problem giving you the toy and playing with you, but you have to play by my rules." Yanking or prying it out of her mouth isn't teaching her anything and will not work as a long-term solution with most dogs.

7. Keep your throws short; the number of reps is more important at this stage, so toss the toy a few feet. As your dog runs to get it, run alongside her but slightly behind her, so as not to distract her from the moving toy. Some dogs will pick up the toy at this point, but others need a little encouragement—you might have to point to the toy or nudge it. Then after your dog picks up the toy, get some eye contact with her, bolt back to the point of origin, and encourage her to chase you. Most energetic dogs love to chase; that is reinforced by your insistence that yours chase you. (Tug-of-war and "let go" are the first two components to teaching fetch; chase is the third.) Once you get that down pat, then run halfway with your dog and encourage her to keep going after the toy. Eventually, you'll run 25 percent of the distance, and then you won't have to run at all.

Training Principle #3: Learning to Communicate

From the second you start training your dog, you need to establish some basic communication with one another. Luckily, dogs are hardwired for that, more so than any other known living being. Brian Hare, PhD, associate professor of evolutionary anthropology at Duke University and coauthor of *The Genius of Dogs*, once said, "Of all the species on this planet, the one that has the gift of reading intentions and understanding what it is that we want to communicate . . . it's in dogs. It's not in chimpanzees and bonobos, our closest relative. It's actually that dogs really do have cognitive abilities to understand us in a way that some species don't."[10]

If you have a puppy or a new dog with little training, then you'll need to accept that it can take some time to establish mutual communication. That's why controlling the environment is vital during this communication building phase, because your dog has yet to learn what you expect of her. This process might feel like it's taking longer than it should, but don't give up—it can take a week or two to lay some groundwork. Once you do, progress will start to speed up quickly.

Here's what you need to know to effectively communicate with your dog:

EYE CONTACT

Eye contact can play a huge role in communication. Dogs make eye contact with us to gather information about our emotions, when and where they might get fed, or what's going on in a particular situation.[11] Researchers have also found that dogs can follow our gaze and even understand the meaning behind it.[12]

Of course, I'm not telling you to stare your dog down—it's just a matter of looking at her in the same way you'd look at another person. *Understanding the training bubble—the distance between your eyes and your dog's eyes—will go a long way when teaching your dog eye contact at first: the closer your eyes are to hers, the faster your dog will likely respond.* I even recommend sitting on the ground when teaching at first so you can really get eye level with your dog. Over time, you can "stretch" that bubble and the distance between you. However, do that slowly or the bubble will pop. More on eye contact and how to teach "look at me" on page 122, chapter 6.

HAND SIGNALS

Think about it—if you met someone who didn't know your language, you might use a lot of hand signals to communicate with one another initially. Well, it's the same thing with dogs. They might have no idea what we're saying at first, and they'll never fully understand everything we say, but hand signals and body language help communicate what we want. That's why when teaching dogs, I always point, gesture, and use exaggerated body language in addition to using words and encouragement. Some dogs are more responsive to hand signals than words, and vice versa—time will tell which one your dog prefers—but in the beginning be sure to incorporate a lot of body language. Feel free to make up any hand signals you'd like!

Don't take it for granted that dogs understand our hand signals—they're able to do so in a way no other species can. As Dr. Hare explains, "In direct comparisons between dogs and apes, dogs are more skilled at using human gestures to find hidden food or objects." For instance, he and other researchers found that if you take two cups and put a treat under one of them and then point to it or even gaze at it, a dog is more likely than a chimpanzee to go toward the correct cup. Researchers have ruled out the possibility that dogs simply use their sense of smell to find the food—the dogs actually follow the humans' gestures to locate the correct cup.[13]

"We have interpreted this to mean that dogs understand the communicative intentions of humans in a way that chimpanzees do not," says Dr. Hare. "It seems dogs are remarkable for their ability to understand our gestures in a flexible way."

TEACHING YOUR LANGUAGE

The average dog's ability to understand our vocabulary is on a par with that of a young child, so don't hold back when it comes to teaching your dog your language. When you're ready to teach your dog what a word means—and that when you say it, you'd like to see a specific action—it's important to keep a few things in mind. Let's take "down" as an example (as in "lie down," not related to jumping): say it once not "Down, down, down, down." There are two problems with repeating a word multiple times: First, your dog might think the word you're saying is actually "Downdowndowndown." Second, even if your dog does eventually learn that you are simply repeating "down" four times, she might interpret that as a precedent to regularly wait until you get to the fourth request. There *are* exceptions to this: for instance, you might occasionally give a request (say, "down") and then repeat it once for emphasis if you want your dog to remain in that position longer than a few seconds ("Yes, down!") However, that's quite different from saying the word you're teaching repeatedly on a regular basis. Instead, be clear and concise. If your dog does not do the thing you've taught her, simply say "No," and then withhold the reward. You might just need to take a break. Also, keep in mind that teaching basic vocabulary can take a few weeks.

When first teaching a word to a dog, it's also important to say the word *after* she performs the skill. So using the example of "down," encourage your dog into a down position using a lure and hand signals (as I explain on page 125, chapter 6). The second she lies down, give her a treat and *then* say "Down!" slowly, one time at a normal volume (no need to shout) and with purpose.

LEARNING YOUR DOG'S COMMUNICATION CUES

Teaching our dogs to understand us is important, but it's just as important that we learn to understand them. A relationship is a two-way street! Anyone who has ever lived with a dog knows that the different barks, growls, and whines they make and their various expressions all mean something. I'd bet that you could probably differentiate between your dog's bark that means a stranger is approaching and a playful bark or one that indicates hunger.

Also, dogs express how they're feeling through their body language, just as we do. Certain dog postures and movements can help you tell the difference between a growl that says "Let's play!" and one that says "Back away." What your pet's body language means will vary based on the individual dog and the actual situation. For example, my dog Alpha Centauri will stand still like a statue with a closed mouth and an intense stare. Outsiders might interpret this as a sign of aggression. However, in my dog's case, it almost always means, "Please, I will do anything if you'll just throw a toy for me right now." Context is *everything*.

Keeping in mind the importance of getting to know *your* dog's cues and the circumstances under which they occur, here are some things to look for in general:

- **Tail:** When it's upright, that usually indicates interest; if it's wagging side to side in combination with other body language that appears to be happy, that probably means the dog's excited or wants to play. Slow, deliberate wags could mean the dog is uncertain about a situation, while a tail tucked between the dog's legs may indicate fear and anxiety.

- **Ears:** When these are pulled back, a dog may be fearful or anxious, relaxed, or simply listening to what's behind her; when pricked forward, the dog is probably on high alert or very interested in something.

- **Eyes:** As you get to know your dog, you'll instantly be able to assess her mood and get an idea of what she might be thinking by looking into her eyes. If you notice her pupils are dilated, her eyes are darting from side to side, or you see the whites of her eyes, she may be afraid of something. A direct, intense stare may indicate a threat or a strong desire to interact with you, but remember there are exceptions to this.

- **Mouth:** Scared dogs may keep their mouths closed or have their teeth bared and lips curled. A dog who is feeling anxious may pant and lick her lips often. However, a dog whose mouth is open with her tongue out is possibly playful or relaxed (though if she's panting, that could mean she's either uneasy or overheated).

- **Posture:** While shy or scared dogs may crouch low to the ground, confident ones may stand tall. If a dog seems natural and relaxed, this probably means she's easygoing in that setting.

Training Principle #4: Be Consistent

The hallmark of any truly successful dog trainer is consistency. Until you get good at this, your dog will not listen to you or understand you in the way that you probably want. I can't overemphasize this point. Yes, it takes some effort to be consistent, but it's really not that difficult.

For example, if you ask your dog to "come" and she doesn't, then it's on you to snap into training mode for a few seconds or minutes and motivate her to come to you, regardless of what you are busy doing. You gave the request; now see it through and make sure you get the result you want. You may have to grab a treat and lure your dog every step of the way from where you called her from or possibly escort her on a leash, but this is what it means to be consistent.

Also, when something happens that you don't like, then it's *your* mandate to make sure it doesn't happen again. Every instance in which your dog performs an action you don't want means it will take more time to resolve. Say your dog rushes into another room after you've asked her to stay, and you don't call her back and repeat this training exercise. You've made an error in your consistency, which may eventually snowball into a dog who listens and responds to requests only on occasion. If you notice that your puppy is chewing on the table leg, you need to divert her attention to something else that is acceptable to chew on *every single time*. (See page 151, chapter 7, for the troubleshooting section on chewing.) In a nutshell, be relentlessly consistent, and I promise you'll get great results.

Training Principle #5: Control the Environment

Again, the number one mistake made by new pet parents is giving their dogs too much freedom too early by not controlling their environment enough! *This is absolutely essential to effective training.* Don't just wing it—dogs are very smart, but without guidance from us, they have no idea how to interact in our culture.

When I have a new dog, my protocol is to attach a four- to six-foot leash to my belt loop during the day so that when I get up to go to the kitchen, check the mail, or do yard work, my dog is with me. This not only allows you to prevent your dog from inquiring about the expensive shoes you left by the front door but also gives you the opportunity to avert or interrupt potential behaviors you don't wish to see repeated. Most important, it also gives you many more opportunities to notice your dog doing things you like so that you can communicate your pleasure with her! For best results, attach your dog to you or make sure she's in a puppy-proofed area the first few weeks or months of training. That way bad habits won't even get started. Your goal is to put your dog in a setting where she is not able to do something you don't want.

Training Principle #6: Train from the Inside Out

If you want long-term meaningful results with your dog, your goal should be not to make your dog do something (which I call "outside-in training") but to make your dog *want* to do something on her own (called "inside-out training").

The idea behind outside-in training is that if you make your dog's life momentarily unpleasant, you will discourage certain behavior in the future. This strategy is called "experiential avoidance," and I find it less than ideal. As I've explained, traditional dog trainers focus on correcting behavior through outside influences including leash jerking, manhandling, and devices such as metal choke chains or prong collars that when quickly popped or jerked around a dog's neck cause discomfort (or outright pain), as a way to communicate "Don't do that." These trainers actually bank on a dog's misbehaving or messing up just so they can teach her a lesson. This is an amateurish, antiquated approach. Remember, we are capable of communicating with dogs much more intelligently than this.

There are many problems with outside-in training. First and foremost, it does nothing to promote the bond between a person and a dog—a bond that is vital during the training process. To me, that alone is immediate grounds for dismissal of this type of training. I see little point in teaching a dog if you can't both enjoy it. I want the dogs I train to be buzzing and loving life to the max—not just because I respect them, but also because I know that's how they learn best.

What's more, outside-in training rarely if ever leads to long-lasting results, as I explained on page 74 in this chapter. Physically forcing your dog to do something—even if it's as simple and benign as pushing her behind down into a sit position—doesn't teach her in a meaningful way that encourages her to think for herself. It's simply too shallow a way to teach a complex animal like a dog. I'm not saying not to touch your dog ever during training—for instance, if she ever needs assistance getting out of the pool, by all means help her! I'm just saying that you shouldn't rely on physically controlling her as a primary training strategy if you want the best results.

Inside-out training, on the other hand, encourages our dogs to use their sophisticated brains. When they *do* think for themselves and behave a certain way because they've been taught to do so by you, then they'll more likely repeat that behavior of their own accord. You'll also see results a lot faster, and your dog will be more prepared for the years ahead.

So how do you get your dog to think from the inside out? Along with learning how to bond and communicate with your dog, it's a matter of showing your dog the right thing to do and then making her life awesome when she does it by rewarding her with a treat and/or playtime, and genuine praise. Stop and think how you felt as a child when an authority figure gave you sincere praise. Maybe you aced a test and your teacher announced that you had the highest score in the class. I'd bet you tried extra hard to have a repeat performance. I know that I certainly advanced faster as a child when my parents or teachers cheered me on and recognized my accomplishments. That's what we want to do with our dogs.

Inside-out training also addresses the *cause* of a problem, not the symptom. For instance, if your dog is chewing a table leg, applying bitter-tasting sprays isn't going to stop your dog from wanting to chew. She may avoid *that* table leg until the spray wears off, but she hasn't learned not to chew up your house and possessions. Tools such as these are just bandages, but they don't get to the root of the issue (which in the case of chewing is most likely boredom or teething). You'll see that everything I'll teach is geared toward addressing the cause, and this will make all the difference.

ASK *Zak*

Stubbornness

"I'm not sure what to think when my dog relieves herself in the house even though she knows she shouldn't, or when I call her to me and she doesn't budge. Is she being stubborn?"

I hear this all the time, and I get it—dogs and especially puppies do things we wish they wouldn't, especially if we let our guard down. Potty accidents are inevitable. Puppy biting sets off even the most patient people. Also, dogs may seem to understand a concept such as "sit" or "come," but they don't always do it when you ask.

I understand why some people automatically blame their dog and say she's being stubborn, but don't do it. In cases when your dog does something you don't like, *you* need to figure out how not to make the mistake again that led to the unwanted behavior. For example, if your dog has a potty accident in the house, that means she is not fully housetrained yet. What do we do when a baby goes in her diaper? We change the diaper and move on because we know that the baby has not had enough time to learn to do otherwise. In the case of your dog, you should clean up the accident, take her out more often for longer periods of time, and do a better job of supervising her or putting her in an environment, such as in a crate, where she is unlikely to repeat the behavior. Getting mad at your dog and, in turn, yelling at her or physically disciplining her in any way is not going to help and threatens to compromise the most important part of training, the bond between you. If you've already done this, just get back on track—dogs don't hold grudges easily and will likely move on quickly. Just remember that any mistakes your dog makes are most likely a sign that you need to do more training and spend more time building communication.

Same goes for when your dog doesn't perform a behavior you ask her to do. So if she doesn't come when you call her, focus on the fundamentals again. *The best trainers in the world are those who take a step back in their training without hesitation!* For instance, your dog might come when you're a few feet away from her at home but not from a greater distance or when there are distractions. Remember, dogs don't quickly generalize a concept, and when there's a change in a major variable, such as a new environment, they need to relearn the concept at first. Also, your dog may not respond when you ask her to do something because you haven't weaned her off treats appropriately, so she's always expecting one.

Lastly, remember that dogs aren't computers, so you shouldn't expect perfection all the time. In fact, in general you should always focus on progress, not perfection. If you want your dog to, say, chase a ball but she doesn't budge, she may just be exhausted. By not moving, it's as though she's saying, "Sorry, we just got back from that long walk. I'm too tired to play right now." Or maybe you haven't gone through the necessary steps to pique your dog's interest in the toy. It's important to respect that.

Together Time

"When I'm relaxing on the couch at night, my dog doesn't want to snuggle; she prefers to sleep under the coffee table. While she can be playful at times, she mostly likes to keep to herself. Why doesn't she like me?"

Just like humans, dogs are individuals and completely diverse in their personalities. Some are shy, some are outgoing. Some like to be on top of you 24/7; others want their space. I couldn't possibly be more bonded with Venus than I already am; however, she just doesn't like being cuddled. I can give her a pet or a hug, and she enjoys a loving moment for a minute, but then she moves on. When I'm watching TV, she'd prefer to leave the room rather than plop down next to me. She never likes to sleep in bed with me. Supernova, on the other hand, is the total opposite. He is by my side at all times and follows me from room to room. At night, not only does he want to sleep in bed with me, but he also wants to lie smack up against me. I know that doesn't mean Supernova loves me more than Venus does; he's just a different dog.

Even if your dog isn't very demonstrative, that doesn't mean you can't encourage a bit of affection. Again, it's important to cater to your dog's personality. For instance, if she's a more reserved dog, don't try to wrestle with her or play rough. Instead, take a gentle approach and pet her softly. Appreciate your dog's innate personality, and if she just wants to chill out by your feet, know that that's her way of saying, "I want to be with you."

Fetch

"I try playing fetch with my dog, but she doesn't seem to have a good handle on it. What should I do?"

I hear this all the time. Fetch training is a little more involved than most people realize, and it can take a few weeks or considerably longer for your dog to learn it well. Most people give up on fetch training prematurely, but I beg you not to. There's definitely a learning curve. It's like when people test out new video games: At first they may get frustrated and lose interest because they don't "get it." However, once they do, watch out—they're hooked! It's the same thing with fetch. You may run into some roadblocks. For instance, I already explained in this chapter what to do to make sure your dog lets go of the toy when playing fetch. Here are some tips for handling some other common problems:

1. **My dog chases and picks up the toy but doesn't bring it back.** This is a sign you need to dial it back a bit. First, make your throws shorter. When you throw the toy and your dog picks it up, start running in the opposite direction and be animated. This will encourage your dog to chase you toward the point of origin. Gradually decrease the distance you are running in the opposite direction until she stops where you ideally want her to stop.

2. ▶ **My dog plays for a few throws but seems to get bored.** This is very normal. One option is to give your dog a five- to twenty-minute break and then try playing fetch again. She may just need a breather. Also, try dialing it up a notch with the enthusiasm—jump around, wave the toy in the air, and do whatever you can to make that toy and yourself seem like *a lot* of fun. Forget about your dignity! Remember, it takes time for dogs to become addicted to fetch; trust me, soon yours will probably never want to stop!

3. **My dog plays fetch inside but never outside.** Changing your dog's surroundings will throw her off in almost any area of training, and that includes fetch. Plus, when you're outside there are so many distractions that can monopolize your dog's attention—a car whizzing by, new smells, another dog barking in the distance, a stick lying in the grass. The key here is to reteach fetch in the new environment and know that while some dogs may pick it up again quickly, others might take a few weeks. Also, when you first go outside, let your dog become acclimated to the new environment and explore around a little bit. That way she can satisfy her curiosity and then get into the game of fetch.

4. **I've tried playing fetch with my dog dozens of times. She really doesn't like it. Do you have any other options?** While fetch is the ideal exercise to help stimulate your dog mentally and physically, I understand that not every dog out there is ultimately going to be a fan of it. However, you've got to let your dog burn off some energy if you expect her to behave and concentrate during training sessions, especially if she's high-energy. Some other options include long hikes, agility courses, and swimming.

CHAPTER FIVE

HOUSETRAINING 101: THE FIVE BASIC RULES

Your new dog is precious, and you feel like that little guy can do no wrong—that is, until he's peed all over your new carpet. Twice! Trust me, I get it. Housetraining, especially for puppies, can be extremely exasperating. Just when you think you're making progress (no accidents for three days!), you step in a puddle right in the middle of your kitchen floor. Don't underestimate the effort it takes to housetrain a dog.

Keep in mind that if you become overly frustrated you're only going to delay progress, and the best way to avoid frustration is by setting realistic expectations: housetraining can take weeks, even months, to really perfect. Please don't correlate difficulty with housetraining with your dog's intelligence. It's not his fault if he doesn't know where to go potty—dogs don't instinctively understand that they should wait to go outside when they have to relieve themselves. In their eyes, this concept is highly unnatural, so you need to patiently teach it to them over time.

Think of housetraining a dog in the same way you'd potty train a child—the more effort you put in up front, the faster you'll achieve success. Whether you have a puppy or an adult dog, remain vigilant for six straight months, no matter how well you think it's going. Just when you think you're getting somewhere, you can experience a major setback if you become overly confident and let your guard down. I've seen this happen with my students more often than you can imagine.

It's unfortunate so many dogs wind up in shelters when people get fed up with housetraining issues because with a little training that scenario is highly preventable. The key to success is understanding that, barring medical issues, you can and *will* housetrain your dog. And as long as you're very consistent, it really doesn't have to be that difficult. In this chapter, I'll teach you what you need to know to get through this important stage of training.

THE FIVE BASIC RULES OF HOUSETRAINING

Here are the steps you'll need for housetraining success.

1. Controlling Environment

In chapter 4, I explained that managing your dog's environment at all times is one of the fundamentals of my training program. When it comes to housetraining, this is far and away the most important key to success. It definitely won't work if you let your dog wander wherever he wants to, right off the bat.

One fact that really helps with housetraining is that dogs instinctively don't like to soil their living area—though, as I'll explain in this section, their idea of a "living area" may be different from yours. This is why a crate can play a key role in housetraining—because it's a comfortable, safe place where your dog can relax and sleep, he's not going to want to have accidents in it. (There may be exceptions to this in the first two weeks or so.) It's where your pet will spend time—in addition to other smallish areas such as a bathroom or puppy playpen—when you can't supervise him. See page 59, chapter 3, to learn how to introduce the crate properly.

You also need to gradually, slowly, and separately teach your dog that other parts of the house are also his living space and, in turn, off limits for going potty. Initially, your dog won't understand this. It's as though he'll think, "Well, I won't go in my crate, but my mother's closet looks perfectly fine. I never really spend any time in there at all!" Start small: for instance, limit your dog's territory to just the kitchen for a short period of time. Then slowly move on to another part of the house. I typically recommend doing this with your dog on leash, though if you're 100 percent focused on your dog you can take the leash off. By paying close attention, you'll likely be able to catch those subtle clues that he's about to go and quickly whisk him outside. Letting him roam off leash in the living room while you keep one eye on him and one on your Facebook newsfeed just isn't what you want to be doing here.

As your dog spends time in each new environment and gets acclimated to it, he'll start realizing that the entire house is his home and not a good choice for going potty. This is a months-long process, one that you shouldn't try to rush. If you notice that your dog is having a lot of accidents, that's a cue to take a step back and refocus on a smaller living space and more frequent potty breaks. Also, if your dog seems to favor various floor textures for going potty, such as carpet or tile, then that's because he's had too many opportunities to do so and has likely developed a preference for them. Prioritize getting him outside more often to encourage a preference for grass!

If crate training is not for you for any reason, then consider alternative ways to contain your dog, such as a playpen, baby gates, or a puppy-proofed room like a bathroom or laundry room. Again, the key is to completely control your dog's environment—if you tether him to you or keep him in his crate or other sectioned-off area any time you can't actively supervise him, then he can't sneak off and go potty in the bedroom.

2. The Importance of Routine

Dogs thrive on a consistent schedule. Plus, keeping a routine is a crucial element to housetraining because it helps you know when your dog will likely have to go out. That starts with feeding your dog at around the same times every day and removing his bowl between meals. Dogs typically will have to go potty about fifteen to twenty minutes after eating. Also, make sure you remove your dog's water dish two hours before bedtime during housetraining.

How often should your dog go outside during the housetraining phase? Very often! In general, one-month-old dogs can hold it in for one hour, two-month-olds for two hours, and so on. However, regardless of your puppy or dog's age, you shouldn't expect him to hold it in longer than three or four hours while he's housetraining. If you work outside of the house all day, either come home periodically during the day to walk your dog, make arrangements for someone else to do this, or consider doggy daycare. Paper training is also an option if you want to do that long term—more on that later in this chapter.

At the very least, walk your dog first thing in the morning, right after he wakes up from a nap, ten to twenty minutes after eating or drinking, after playtime, and right before bedtime. With a puppy, you will also likely need to get up in the middle of the night once or twice to let him out for that first week or two.

When you walk your dog outside, never leave him unsupervised. It's important for you to be there to praise him and reward him for doing his business outside. When I housetrain dogs, I will generally say something like, "Do you want to go potty?" *before* I let them out. I then let them out in the yard, on leash, so that I can guide them to a specific area and remain very quiet. Don't be surprised if your dog checks out the yard and sniffs around or tries to play for a few minutes first. This is normal. It's best to wait it out and ignore your dog's efforts to play. (However, this applies to potty breaks only! In other areas of training, it's very helpful if your dog wants to play and engage with you.)

Spend a good ten minutes out there with your dog if necessary. Ten minutes can seem like thirty, so adjust your expectations. If your dog goes potty, say "Yes!" and then after a one-second pause say "Go potty!" as he is finishing up. Be very deliberate and purposeful in your tone, as though you are teaching a new phrase to a young child. No need to be loud or say this a dozen times. Once is just fine. Then promptly follow the phrase up with a reward and genuine encouragement right there outside (more on rewards in the next section).

If your dog doesn't go potty after ten minutes, then bring him back into the house and put him in the crate or other small contained environment he likely views as his living area, or keep him tethered to you. Try taking him out again ten to fifteen minutes later, or sooner if you see signs that he has to go, such as circling and sniffing the ground. This may sound like a lot of work, but trust me—the more committed you are to frequent bathroom breaks initially, the sooner your dog will get the hang of housetraining.

3. The Power of Rewards

Creating positive associations with housetraining is very important so that your dog will *want* to go potty outside. In other words, give your dog a special reward to look forward to after he uses the proper spot. I'm not saying you have to do this every day for the rest of his life—just during housetraining. Such rewards come in two major forms: food or play.

For food, treats that your dog *loves* will work well. Again, a small piece of real meat like boiled chicken really gets a dog's attention. Another option: if your dog is very playful, you can instead encourage a five- to thirty-second play session immediately after he goes potty. A play session can be defined as anything that your dog really enjoys, like chasing you around, playing tug-of-war, or a game of fetch. The idea here is to have fun!

No matter which reward you choose, while you are waiting for your dog to go potty, stay boring and hide any toys or treats. After he goes, *then* reward him and praise him lavishly. Just pretend like you've won the lottery every time he is successful outside, and he'll start realizing that he just did something that resulted in life getting way more interesting. For a more sensitive or nervous dog, you may want to tone down the excitement a bit. Otherwise, lay it on thick!

Bottom line: Your goal is to teach your dog that going potty outside unlocks the most fun version of you—*plus* a special surprise! This may take several days to a few weeks for your dog to understand. Once he does, you can bet that housetraining will become a lot easier.

4. Handling Accidents

You should never punish your dog for having a potty accident. Doing that is like punishing an infant for going in his diaper. Old-school training encouraged pushing a dog's face into his mess or even hitting him with a newspaper—I can't think of a quicker way to not only compromise your dog's trust but also greatly delay his progress. As I've been emphasizing, if you want the best results, focus on what you like instead of what you don't like.

When you catch your dog in the act of going in the house, interrupt him immediately by distracting him with a high-pitched voice or by clapping your hands and take him outside to finish up. Then reward him heavily for doing so in the right spot. If you don't catch him in the act, scolding him after the fact is counterproductive. Instead, just clean up the mess and make sure you're supervising your dog as much as possible to prevent future accidents. Remember, your dog is not to blame here. The only thing to blame is the lack of a controlled environment or your consistency.

5. Cleaning Up

When your dog has an accident in the house, do your best to eliminate odors; if you don't, your dog will be drawn to those spots over and over again. Dogs like to go potty where they and other dogs have done so before. Even though you may not be able to see or smell a stain after you clean it up, your dog can detect it with his extremely sensitive sense of smell. Look for an enzyme-based odor neutralizer that breaks down the scent. You can find such products at pet supply stores, online, and in some grocery stores. Do not use ammonia, vinegar, detergents, or other similar chemicals. They aren't effective, and they also may attract your dog back to the spot.

A WORD ABOUT WALKING ON A LEASH

One of the biggest complaints I get from my clients is that their dogs pull on the leash. I understand how frustrating that can be, let alone difficult to control. However, when you're housetraining, the potty breaks themselves are not the time to teach your dog not to pull on a leash. Dogs can learn many things at one time, but the concepts of housetraining and walking slowly are both so highly unnatural and nonintuitive to dogs that they should be taught very separately.

Also, you can't just teach your dog perfect leash walking during regularly scheduled walks when you have a certain destination or a time limit. You'll need to dedicate separate training sessions for this. For now, when you walk your dog the focus should be specifically on getting him to go potty outside and rewarding him heavily when he does. Don't worry; your dog will walk properly on a leash soon enough (I'll explain how to train him to do that in the next chapter). However, I'm guessing that your top priority right now is to make sure he doesn't ruin every carpet in your house!

ASK *Zak*

Paper Training

"I live in a high-rise in New York City, so rushing out to walk my puppy is a lot easier said than done. Can I teach him to go on a pad in my house?"

I generally discourage paper training (also known as puppy pad training) if your ultimate goal is to have your dog relieve himself outside. It's an unnecessary step. If you start with pads but go on to introduce grass, you will likely confuse your dog and have to retrain him to go outside. In these cases, just start with the grass right off the bat.

However, if you plan on *always* using pads, based on your living arrangements or other circumstances, then that's fine. For example, if you live on the thirtieth floor in a building, then you may want your dog to go on pads indefinitely—it can be difficult for some dogs to hold it while waiting for an elevator, and it certainly can be a nuisance for you.

One caveat: If you live in an urban area, your vet may recommend not walking your dog on the street until he's gotten all his shots, since the chances your dog will pick up a virus or infection in a crowded city such as New York or Boston are much higher than they are, say, on your front lawn in the suburbs. In these cases, you can start with pads and then make the switch—just understand that you're going to have to reteach your dog when you do. If your dog is having trouble with the transition, it may help to bring a pad outside, since he's already comfortable going on that texture. Be patient! Asking your dog to do something in a new environment, in this case outside, will almost inevitably throw him off. Eventually, he'll catch on and you can remove the pad; it just might take some time.

For paper training, the same rules apply as with regular housetraining, except instead of taking your dog outside every hour, you'll walk him to the puppy pads. As soon as he goes, praise him, give him a reward, remove the soiled pad, and replace it with a new one (though if you've just begun housetraining it can't hurt to leave a pad soiled with urine in place for a few days so the smell encourages him to go). Some people who want their dogs to go inside opt to use dog litter boxes, some of which even use real or synthetic grass. If you're interested in this option, check out your local pet supply store or online retailers.

Crate Training

"I know dogs aren't supposed to soil their sleeping area, but my puppy just went in his crate. What do I do about this?"

It's common for young puppies to have accidents in their crate at first—they may have no idea that their crate is their "bedroom" and the area they shouldn't soil. Minimize these accidents by taking your dog outside more often. As your dog comes to realize that the crate is his own cozy living and sleeping space, you should begin to see these instances dwindle and eventually stop altogether within a few days or weeks.

Sadly, some dogs think they *should* do their business in their crate because that's all they know—for instance, dogs from puppy mills or pet stores, or dogs who were previously in the care of a neglectful person may have spent most if not all of their time in a crate and had no choice but to relieve themselves there. Even these dogs can be rehabilitated; however, it will likely require some extra patience on your part. Of course, if your dog seems either overly anxious about the crate or very comfortable going potty in it, you should consider other ways to contain him when you can't supervise him as I mentioned earlier.

When it comes to housetraining, there are no absolutes. Even when a dog is fully trained and knows not to go in his crate, he can still have accidents if he's left in there too long. Remember, dogs under six months or any dog who is in the process of housetraining typically shouldn't spend more than three or four hours at a time in the crate. Puppies simply can't hold it in, and older dogs need to first learn that they should do so.[1]

Excitement/Submissive Urination

"Every time the doorbell rings, my dog pees on the floor. What's up with that?"

Excitement urination/submissive urination is when a dog becomes nervous or excited, loses control of his bladder, and accidentally urinates. Sometimes it can be a few drops; other times it can be enough to create quite a puddle. Excitement urination may occur when your dog becomes elated to see you when you come home, while he's playing, or anytime someone visits. It's very common in puppies, and most dogs outgrow it by their first birthday.

Submissive urination has the same result, but dogs do it for a different reason: they are conveying nervousness or fear related to a person, another dog, or a situation. If you yell at your dog (which I *never* recommend) and he immediately pees on the floor, that's most likely submissive urination. Also, many dogs are just naturally shy and more prone to submissive urination no matter how sweet you are to them. Again, this is normal in puppies. I just need to clarify that though the term for this kind of peeing is "submissive urination," we are not talking about "submissive" as opposed to "dominance." As I've explained before, the whole concept of dog-to-human dominance is a myth.

First things first: Visit your vet to rule out an underlying medical issue such as a urinary tract infection or urinary incontinence. If that's not the cause, then it's time to work on reducing the behavior.

Remember, though, this behavior is involuntary, so you'll need to be extra understanding. Here are tips for handling both kinds of accidents:

- Since this behavior is somewhat predictable—for example, you know you your dog is likely to pee when guests arrive—then take your dog out before a visitor is expected.

- General socialization will likely reduce this behavior dramatically. As new situations become less of an event for your dog, he will be less excited or nervous. (See page 61, chapter 3, to learn how to properly socialize your dog.)

- As with general housetraining, never punish your dog or yell at him for submissive or excitement urination. Doing so will not help the situation at all; it may only make the problem worse.

- To help your dog with submissive peeing, make sure that when you approach him you don't do so with a posture that he might view as confrontational. No yelling or grabbing! Instead, encourage him to approach you, perhaps by using a treat or fun toy he likes, so that he feels more confident. Overall, the rule of thumb here is to be extra gentle.

- To help with excitement peeing, make any introductions or greetings as mellow as possible. That means when you walk through the door don't start playing an immediate game of chase, talking in a high-pitched voice, and getting your dog all riled up. Instead, ignore him until you can get him outside to go potty. Guests should follow the same protocol.

Regression

"My dog has been housetrained for months, but all of a sudden he's been having accidents in the house. Why would he be doing this?"

Relapses in housetraining are very normal and expected. As with all things in dog training, you don't go from A to Z, letter by letter, start to finish. Instead, you'll make some progress, you'll experience a few slipups, and then you'll make a little more progress. It's less of a linear process than most people realize, so prepare to stay the course.

If your dog seemed to have housetraining down pat and suddenly starts having accidents, first take him to the vet to rule out any medical issues such as a bladder infection, a gastrointestinal problem, or a urinary tract infection. If none of those are the cause, then here are some other possible culprits:

- **A new environment.** Just because your dog learns not to go in your house does not mean he will generalize this behavior to other areas. If you move, visit a friend's house, or leave him with a relative while you go out of town, you may need to reteach your dog the potty rules in these new places.

- **A change in the family.** A dog may regress if you add a partner or child to the mix. The same is true if you add another pet (or if you lose one).

- **Added stress.** Anything that causes anxiety in your dog can lead to housetraining regression—from suddenly switching the place where he sleeps to introducing a new routine.

How to get back on track? If your dog has already established a habit of relieving himself inside, be extra patient and take a big step back in your training. Limit his access to various parts of the house by either keeping him on leash and tethered to you when you are home or putting him in a contained setting when you cannot supervise him. Obviously, letting your dog out of your sight is unacceptable if you hope to get this done in a reasonable amount of time. Don't worry, though; whenever you are trying to reestablish a good habit that you've had success with in the past, you'll see results faster than you did initially.

Night Waking

"My puppy is five months old and I'm still getting up with him a few times each night to walk him. Is this normal, and when will I ever get a good night's sleep again?"

If your new dog is crying and keeping you up for more than two weeks straight, ask your vet if there might be an underlying medical condition that is causing the night waking. If not, then think of yourself as a new parent with a baby and get your dog on a sleep schedule.

First, remember that nothing encourages a dog to sleep through the night like proper exercise during the day. The more often you can thoroughly exercise your dog before bed with age-appropriate exercise, the better! Discourage long naps throughout the day by doing what you can to keep your dog engaged. Lots of training will also encourage a good night's sleep. Have you ever studied for a test all day? You'll understand that this type of mental activity requires you to recharge, too.

Also, you'll need to know the difference between a whine that means, "I really have to go potty" and a whine that means, "Let me out of here because I feel like playing at 3 A.M." You'll learn these nuances as you get to know your dog better—I find that the "I have to go potty" whine is a quiet, yet urgent whimper, while the "Let's play" whine is more insistent, often with some barking. If you can't tell the difference, give it a few days; you'll understand what I mean. Lastly, if your dog is demanding to be let out and you know he doesn't have to go, just ignore the behavior, provided he's not overly stressed out. Eventually, he'll realize that his fussing isn't getting him anywhere, and he'll likely fall asleep.

Ringing a Bell

"I know some people teach their dogs to ring a bell when they have to go out. That sounds great. Do you recommend it?"

This is a clever trick, and there's nothing wrong with teaching it to your dog, but I don't recommend that you rely on this for housetraining. Your dog has so much to learn at first, and trying to teach your dog this trick is simply an unnecessary step. Instead, you should have your dog on a solid schedule and not insist that he tells you when he needs to go out. This is too much responsibility for your dog during the housetraining process. It is your job to let him out often before he even realizes he has to go. Once your dog is almost fully housetrained, you'll start to notice his subtle cues, such as walking to the door, becoming restless or animated, sniffing the ground, and circling. Dogs are great at communicating when they want something!

Scent Marking

"I just adopted a second dog, and now both my dogs are peeing all over my house. What is going on?"

Some dogs will scent mark by urinating on objects, typically vertical ones such as a fire hydrant, tree, or table leg, often by raising a leg. This behavior usually starts between six months and two years. Unneutered male dogs are most likely to exhibit this behavior, though neutered male dogs and females may do so as well. Dogs may mark because they smell another dog's urine in the area or because they're anxious or excited; some males do it only in the presence of females, whereas others do it only in the presence of other males or by themselves.

Many dogs who mark will do so only outside of the home. However, if you're bringing another pet into your house, one or both dogs might start marking other areas of the house. A dog also might do this if you add a new person to the household, such as a partner or a new baby.

So what can you do? In general, I recommend that my clients first make sure the marking isn't due to a medical condition. Also, if your dog hasn't been spayed or neutered yet, talk to your vet about doing so, as that may help reduce the behavior. However, keep in mind that training should always be your "plan A" to resolve this. Never punish your dog for marking in the house, and always clean up any mess immediately with an enzyme-based odor neutralizer.

Next, take a step back on your training and limit your dog's access to the entire house in favor of small areas at a time. Supervise vigilantly and look for those subtle signs that your dog is thinking about marking, such as sniffing and circling, so that you can preempt that behavior by promptly taking your dog outside. It can't hurt to walk your dog more often than usual. Also, if your dog seems to be reacting to a new person or pet in the house, work on establishing a good relationship between them. For instance, if you're bringing in a new roommate, she might want to spend time playing with your dog, feeding him, and caring for him in other ways.

Accidents After a Walk

"Sometimes I'll walk my dog for twenty minutes, and he doesn't go potty. However, within minutes of coming back home he goes all over the floor. What am I doing wrong?"

This usually means one of two things: either your dog has not equated outside with potty time, or your dog simply prefers to go inside on the carpet, hardwood floors, or tile. Either way, it's easy to correct unwanted behaviors if you think they might happen at a specific time. If you know there's a high probability that your dog will pee in the house within a few minutes of coming back into the house, this means that that particular housetraining session isn't over yet. Be alert and observe your dog until the moment just before he starts doing his business inside, then promptly get him outside! This means rather than repeatedly accepting, "I guess he doesn't have to go, so let's go back inside . . . Aww, rats, you did it again!" instead get into the mindset of, "Okay, let's go inside and hang out near the door so I can promptly get you outside when you squat or sniff the floor, since I know you are likely to behave in this predictable manner."

Home Alone

"My dog seems to be getting the hang of housetraining. Does that mean I can start leaving him in the house unattended?"

In general, I don't advise leaving dogs completely unattended with full run of the house until they're around two, because they can get into a lot of trouble—potty accidents aside, they might destroy your furniture or get into something that can really hurt them. Of course, this varies tremendously from dog to dog, so you have to use your judgment.

When you think your dog is ready to stay home alone out of his crate or confined area, look for opportunities to briefly leave him for a few minutes at a time. Don't wait until it's time to go to work and hope for the best. Instead, leave your dog in the kitchen while you run into the bathroom for a minute or two. If he's successful and doesn't have any accidents, repeat the test a little later that day or the next day. The goal is to gradually increase both the time that your dog is unsupervised and the size of the area that you're leaving him in.

Once your dog is doing well for ten to twenty minutes at a time, you can try actually leaving the house. Next time you run to the grocery store or gas station for a few minutes, for example, test your dog for real by leaving him unattended. If you return and everything went well, that's great news! However, don't think you're safe for the long term yet—this just means your dog passed his initial test. Conversely, if your dog has an accident, take a step back and next time don't leave him alone for so long. Do many tests like this before gradually leaving your dog alone for longer periods.

Housetraining Success

"My dog hasn't had an accident in the house for five weeks. Does that mean housetraining is complete?"

Congratulations! When your dog goes one to two months with absolutely no accidents, and he's able to go several hours between potty breaks, then you are probably out of the woods for the most part. Some older dogs will get there within a week or so; many others, including puppies, can take a few months or even longer to reach this milestone.

However, keep in mind that just because your dog seems to have mastered housetraining, that doesn't mean he'll never slip up again. As I mentioned earlier, dogs can regress for all sorts of reasons, such as illnesses or changes in their environment. If this happens, don't worry— just take a few steps back and start with the basics I've outlined in this chapter. Your dog should be back on track in no time.

CHAPTER SIX

BASIC TRAINING: THE FUNDAMENTAL SKILLS EVERY DOG NEEDS TO KNOW

Once you bring your dog home, you may be wondering when you can start training her. The answer is "Now!" If you have a puppy, you may be astonished at what your dog is capable of learning at a very young age. And if you have an older dog, recall that the cliché "You can't teach an old dog new tricks" is completely untrue. No matter what your dog's age is, she'll be ready to learn from you from day one. Dogs crave human interaction to feel complete—remember, they were bred to work with us.

There are two main types of training sessions: primary ones, in which you attempt to teach something new to your dog, and secondary ones, which are more spontaneous, casual training sessions that arise due to specific circumstances. Either way, here are a few things to keep in mind when you start training:

- **Don't expect unrealistically fast results.** Sure, your dog will learn some things like "sit" very quickly; however, others skills, such as ignoring distractions on a walk, can take much longer. *The slower you go, the faster your results will be.* For the first six to eight weeks, establish a rough draft of the behaviors you want. Then you can spend the next six months to a year refining your dog's behavior to a point that fits your family's lifestyle, needs, and ultimate goals.

- **You won't have linear, successive progress.** You will have a few bumps in the road, and that's perfectly normal. Do you remember ever learning a concept in school and feeling like you understood it, but when you got home and had to do homework related to that concept you were totally lost? Dogs seem to experience the same thing.

- **Never blame your dog.** Remember that when you minimize *your* mistakes, your dog will learn faster.

- **Dogs learn best *after* exercise.** One big frustration point for many of my clients is that their dogs won't listen when they introduce new concepts. That's primarily because most people with hyper dogs don't know to exercise their dogs before primary training sessions. *Remember, dogs like this cannot absorb new concepts until they burn off their excess energy.* If you have a dog with lots of energy, engage in a vigorous activity with her, such as fetch, before you start training.

- **Be flexible!** Things are not black-and-white when it comes teaching your dog. It's time to throw out the overgeneralizations about your dog's breed or mix and focus on her as an individual.

REWARDS: THE IMPORTANCE OF KNOWING YOUR DOG'S CURRENCY

Imagine if you were given a bonus at work whenever you did your job well. I'm sure most of you would say that that would definitely give you extra incentive to always try your best. Our dogs have their own version of this. There are two primary types of currency or "money" for your dog: really good treats and, for many dogs, extra playtime. For something to qualify as amazing currency, your dog must absolutely love it, not just like it. Keep in mind that affection doesn't count as currency— our dogs should never be required to earn this, so dish out the love for free, as much as you'd like.

For treats during primary training sessions, again, use tiny pieces of real chicken or other meat. The reward should be the size of a grain of rice for small dogs, and no larger than a pea for medium to large dogs. Trust me, it's the quality of the treat, not the quantity, that counts, because you want to have the option of rewarding over and over again without filling your dog up. Think of this tiny piece of meat as the equivalent of a $1 bill to your dog. What about commercial dog treats? They have their place too, and I suggest having several containers of soft dog treats throughout the house because there will be times when you need to burst into a spontaneous training session and you'll need to have your dog's currency handy. Think of these as equivalent to a quarter. Dog biscuits and even bits of kibble are equivalent to a penny. It's fine to give them to your dog, but not when training. Remember, the currency you choose has to *really* excite your dog.

While great treats will work with most dogs, some moderate- to high-energy dogs will really excel if you reward a training success with a brief play activity, such as a five-second game of tug-of-war or one or two tosses of a ball. I stress this because it's far too common for people to insist that their dog accept that treats be the reward, even as their dog, say, jumps on them and bites at the leash. These are sure signs that a dog is desperately trying to initiate play. If your dog is saying, "I want to do *this*," then try to incorporate whatever that is into the reward. So in the case of biting on the leash during a walk, consider using a tug toy to bring the attention onto an acceptable currency instead. Also, remember to put away your dog's favorite toys unless you are playing with them—that way your pet will be excited when you bring them out as a reward. If special toys like balls, Frisbees, and tug toys are just left out all the time, they'll likely lose their potency.

Do you have to reward with food or play forever? Absolutely not! However, for the first year of training, you want your dog always wondering what she might win if she listens. And for the first sixteen weeks of training, I strongly encourage you to reward your dog liberally—the more you praise and "pay" her, the faster she'll learn. After your dog has fully demonstrated that she understands a particular skill in the environment where you are teaching, you can tone down the rewards by following intermittent reinforcement, which I explained on page 78, chapter 4. Rewarding your dog occasionally with no discernible pattern keeps her guessing—and listening. Use this psychology to your advantage!

Regardless of the reward you use—and you can certainly use both food and play if that works for your dog—always give her a lot of affection and show your appreciation. Don't just be a robot when giving treats and engaging in playtime. Also, don't pay lip service and get excited when your dog does something well only because that's what you're "supposed" to do. You must be *genuinely* encouraging. I remember when my dad taught me how to play baseball when I was a boy. He explained the game to me and told me to keep my eye on the ball and try and hit it when it approached. When I succeeded, he didn't simply say "good" in a monotone voice; he was so excited that he came over, hugged me, and said he was so proud. It was his sincerity and positive energy that I was encouraged by, and I know that dogs are sophisticated enough to be encouraged in the same way.

So what do you treat for? At first, find tiny reasons to reward your dog when introducing a new concept. Open up the bank account and let the money flow. Your dog doesn't have to perfect a skill to get a treat or playtime; even if she makes the slightest move in the right direction or does what you ask for a split second, reward her so she knows she's on the right track. These little moments give you traction as you build communication. You may find yourself rewarding your dog dozens of times a day for such small successes, and that's fine. As I mentioned earlier, that's why you should give a minuscule bit of a treat, nothing big. It's her tastebuds you're trying to please, not her stomach.

▶ CLICKER TRAINING

I am a huge fan of clicker training, and I encourage you to use one if you're interested. The clicker is a small, inexpensive device available from many dog retailers; its clicking sound tells your pet, "Yes! Good dog! I like what you did! You win a prize!" after you've conditioned her to understand this, which can take mere seconds.

I often recommend that beginners use a clicker because it helps them get better with timing, an essential ingredient to dog training that most people are not immediately good at. When first teaching a new concept, I always suggest rewarding for every tiny bit of progress. For instance, if you ask your dog to "watch me" and she does so for even a second, it's important to always let her know she's on the right track. Saying "Yes, I like that, and that, and that" repeatedly can be challenging at first; you may need to do that dozens of times in one session. Sometimes our fingers are quicker than our words, and if you have a clicker in your hand to press at the moment your dog moves toward the behavior you want, you are going to be clearer and more consistent when trying to communicate what you like. Eventually, your dog will look for ways to make that clicker go off, which is exactly what you want!

Here's how to introduce the clicker:

- Don't start with the clicker too close to your dog; the sound makes some dogs anxious at first. It's better to start at a distance or by muffling the sound a bit with your hand.

- Next, click the clicker a single time, wait about a second or two, and give your dog a reward. Do this for a few minutes until your dog seems accustomed to the clicking noise. Be methodical and deliberate, but don't make any type of request with the clicker. You simply want to communicate that when the clicker makes a sound, a small, great-tasting treat will follow.

- Now start incorporating the clicker into actual training. Ask your dog to sit (I'll explain how to teach that a little later in this chapter). The *second* your dog's backside hits the ground, you click, and follow up with a reward. If you tell your dog "Watch me," the second she makes eye contact with you, click and reward. Also, try coupling the click with the word "yes" either directly before or after the click. An awesome thing happens when you do this: your dog will learn that the click and "yes" mean the same thing.

- When teaching a new skill, click only once for each small success and reward each time.

- Eventually, you can wean off the clicker. The clicker is as temporary or as permanent as you'd like it to be.

"YES" AND "NO" IN TRAINING

These two words are the backbone of your initial training. To effectively teach them, it's important that every time you say "Yes" to tell your dog you like something she did, you need to follow this up with a good reward at first. That way the word "yes" means something to your dog—specifically, a treat or a brief play session.

As for "no," please understand that when you say this word to your dog it should never come from a place of anger or frustration. There's no need to raise your voice or be authoritative. "No" should simply mean, "Nope, that's not what I'm looking for here. Please try again!" Every time you say "No" you should also withhold the reward itself or, in the case of your dog's chewing a shoe, you should take the shoe away. This is the consequence for doing something you do not wish to see repeated. You can also remove your dog from the environment when necessary—she can't dig up your carpet when she's in a puppy playpen in the kitchen. Never follow "no" with a leash jerk or other harsh corrections. The key is to teach with decency and logic, not force.

Here's an example of "yes" and "no" in action: Assuming you are confident that your dog knows the word "sit" in the environment you're working in, don't simply repeat "Sit" a second time if your dog doesn't sit when you first ask her to do so. Instead, say "Sit," then wait a few seconds, and if your dog doesn't do it, say "No" as a way of saying "Try again." Then, when your dog does sit, say "Yes, sit!" and reward her so she'll understand that she's done the right thing. The better you get at emphasizing the "yes," the better teacher you'll become!

One more note: In the beginning, sticking with "yes" and "no" may make your job easier, but as you progress you may find yourself using synonyms for these words. If you're more the type to say "Awesome," "Great job," or "Nope," then go with it! I really want you to feel liberated to be natural and real when training, so this is your call.

THE BASIC SKILLS

Here, I'll walk you through the fundamentals all dogs should know.

Supplies Needed:

- A four- to six-foot leash
- A twenty- to thirty-foot lead leash
- A harness and/or a nonmetal collar
- Treats
- A few favorite toys
- A clicker (optional)

A Reminder: Introducing New Words

When you're teaching your dog any skills, remember that you shouldn't just say the word, such as "Come" or "Stay," before you've taught her to do it. Here's what to do:

1. Get your dog to perform the action you intend to pair with a word by either luring her or encouraging her with your body language.

2. As your dog does the thing you like, say "Yes" (or "Awesome," "Good job," or whatever you'd like) and then say the new word or phrase. For example, if you were teaching your dog to stand up on all fours, you would say "Yes, stand!" as your dog stands up, not before. Be deliberate, even taking twice as long as usual to say the word to really emphasize this.

3. As the behavior becomes more reliable, begin preceding the action with the word and a hand signal. When your dog does the behavior, say "Yes" and give a reward.

▶ Watch Me/Look at Me

If you eventually want your dog to focus on you and listen to you in any situation regardless of distractions, you *must* start with teaching your dog "Watch me" (or its variant, "Look at me"). It's so important that it's the very first thing I teach most dogs. If your dog isn't looking at you, then it will be that much more difficult to guide her. Also, having eye contact with your dog is a crucial element to communication, just as it is with other humans. Of course, I'm not saying you should go up to a dog you don't know and stare her in the eyes; some dogs could find that confrontational. This is about learning to connect with *your* dog. Here's what to do:

1. If you are comfortable doing so, sit on the ground so that you're eye level with your dog. Hold a treat directly in front of your eyes. Your dog will likely look at the treat, and as soon as you have eye contact with her, say "Yes, watch me!" Start close, keeping your training bubble—the distance between your dog's eyes and your own—very small. The closer you are to your dog, the more likely she will comprehend what you want at first. Repeat this a few times. Once your dog is reliably looking at the treat as you hold it to your eyes, move on to the next step.

2. Most dogs are very receptive to body language—so next, point to your eyes with your index finger but this time without a treat in your hand. That way your dog is now looking at your finger, not at the food. Again, as soon as she looks at you, say "Yes,

watch me!" and then you can give her a treat with your other hand. Do you see what we did? We taught our first hand signal, and what a powerful one it is! Reward liberally for weeks on this one.

3. Gradually stretch the training bubble by working your way up to being able to stand straight up. The goal is that you'll be able to stand up and hold your dog's gaze for five to ten seconds as she remains in front of you. Once you have your dog's eyes on you, you'll know you have her attention!

▶ Leave It

I can't stress too much how vital this skill is. "Leave it" will be a foundation for distraction training down the road (which I'll cover in a bit), and it can also possibly save your dog's life if she's about to gobble up something she finds on the ground. I promise that you can quickly teach your dog to leave anything alone without touching her or restraining her in any way. Here's what to do:

1. Put a bit of food in your hand. Let your dog know it's there. Your dog will probably frantically try to get to it, especially if she's got a lot of energy, so close your hand at first if necessary to prevent that. After thirty seconds to two minutes, most dogs will either become distracted by something else or will lose interest for a microsecond, which is when you instantly say "Yes," and then after a deliberate half-second pause, say "Leave it" while you immediately give her the food. Repeat this step a few times.

2. Next, slowly place a piece of food on the floor in front of your dog. Again, she will probably lunge for it, so put your hand over the food, restricting her access to it, and say "No." Since saying "No" always has a consequence, in this case the consequence is that she can't have the food. Notice how I'm not suggesting you touch your dog, pull her away from the food, or nudge her backward. Instead, you are encouraging her to think for herself and decide to leave the morsel alone. This is "inside-out" teaching in full bloom.

3. Begin to slowly reveal the food to your dog, making sure you cover it up each time your dog tries to get it prematurely. When your dog doesn't go for it or uses even the slightest bit of self-restraint, enthusiastically say "Yes, leave it!" Give her the reward. However, don't let her eat it off the floor—pick it up and give it to her so she learns that rewards always come directly from you. Repeat this often.

4. As your dog shows that she understands "leave it," begin surprising her with spontaneous, sixty-second "leave it" training sessions to start simulating real-life distractions. Practice this as much as you can. You'll use "leave it" to set up lots of future training sessions, so get really good at it!

Leave It/Watch Me Combo

Now that you've learned "leave it" and "watch me," it's time to combine them. *This is a magical exercise* and one of the most important lessons because it is the first step to teaching your dog to listen to you in the face of distractions. Your dog might leave something alone during a mellow training session in your house, but it's a whole different ballgame getting her to do the same while you're on a walk and she encounters a cat running by, another dog, or a chicken bone on the sidewalk. If you can make it through this exercise (which you will!), you're going to be unstoppable! Here's what to do:

1. Start simply in your home. Do a basic "leave it" drill with a piece of meat. However, this time when your dog leaves the meat alone, encourage her to look at you by saying "Watch me." (Since you've changed a variable here—adding "watch me" to "leave it"—your dog may be thrown off at first, so don't expect a polished result initially.) When she does, say "Yes" and reward her. See what you're doing? You're getting your dog's attention on you instead of on a real piece of meat right in front of her! Dogs must be able to do this before you can expect them to listen to you outside of the house.

2. Mix things up a little bit. Take a favorite toy and drop it in front of your dog. When you drop it, have her repeat the "leave

it/watch me" drill. It's important to practice this as much as possible and in a variety of ways. Work up to throwing the toy or treat as you walk with your dog away from it, toward it, or to the left or right of it. The idea is that you are preparing her for real-life distractions by showing her how to respond to mild distractions at first.

3. If you are doing well with this, move the lesson to your front yard or driveway. Your dog may be thrown off by this significant change at first, so just slow down and don't insist that she do the "leave it/watch me" drill as well as she did inside quite yet.

4. The purpose of this drill is to make sure your dog understands the concept of choosing to look to you even when she sees something she wants. As your dog gets better at this, take the opportunity to practice it in various situations. For example, maybe you see another dog down the street behind a fence. From a distance that is not too overwhelming to your dog, practice "watch me." In essence, the dog in the distance is now the distraction instead of the treat or toy. Of course, perfecting this skill when your dog is really excited about something she sees, hears, or smells may take lots of practice. Low-energy dogs often pick it up quickly because they're less persistent by nature. However, if you have a high-energy dog like I do, work at a faster pace by aiming to get lots of back-to-back successes (even if those successes are very small).

▶ Sit/Down/Up/Stand

Dogs are capable of learning multiple things at once, so in my training classes I always introduce the concepts of "sit," "down," "up," and "stand" in one lesson. I do this by lure training—using a treat to entice your dog to achieve a specific physical position. You're not just tossing a treat to your dog; you're actually using the treat to guide her into the desired position or through a particular motion. This way you can *show your dog how to do what you want* as opposed to *making her do what you want*. Lure training will come in handy in a variety of training circumstances.

To do lure training most effectively, you'll need to remember you're luring with your dog's nose, not her eyes, so think of the treat and your dog's nose as magnets. They need to be very close at all times when initially luring. If a treat and a dog's nose get too far apart, the lure falls apart. Also, nearly all people lure too fast at first. Instead, lure in slow motion. Doing this delivers the fastest results. If your dog does not follow the food lure at first, this likely means you're not using a treat she *loves*, you're moving too fast, or you're asking her to do something in an unfamiliar or distracting environment and she just needs time to adjust. Here's what to do:

1. **Sit:** Hold a small treat between your thumb and forefinger and make sure that your dog sees it. Keeping it very close to your dog's nose, move it up over the bridge of her nose and up so that she lifts her nose directly up toward the ceiling or sky. As her head tilts farther back, usually she will naturally sit down. (If she jumps up, then that probably means you are starting with the treat too high away from her face.) The second your dog's hind legs touch the ground, say "Yes, sit" once, then give her the treat and some enthusiastic praise.

2. **Down:** Next, starting with your dog sitting and keeping the treat "magnetized" to your dog's nose, very slowly move the treat down to the ground so that your dog follows the lure into a down position. When she lies down, say something like "Great job, down" and give her the treat. It's worth noting that some dogs, particularly small ones, do not follow a lure well when going into a "down" specifically. For these dogs, it may help to lure down and inward toward their chests. You also have the option of "capturing" a down. For example, many dogs begin to turn in a circle right before they lie down, giving you notice that they're about to do it. This would be your cue to say "Down" as your dog performs the action. When you rely on capturing behaviors, results may take some extra time, but you'll still get there if you're consistent.

3. **Up:** After starting with "sit" and "down," raise the lure back up so that your dog automatically rises to reach it. This lure can be

farther away from your dog's nose, as most dogs are fairly eager to get the treat (though some might need a little coaxing). Your goal is to get her from the down position to the "sit" position. I call this "up" because the action from the dog's perspective is much different from a usual "sit." When your dog reaches her head up and she rises into a sit position, say "Yes, up" and give her the treat.

4. **Stand:** Now that your dog is back into the sit position, take the lure and move it *slowly* away from her face but slightly upward until she naturally stands up on all fours. Say "That's it! Stand" and give her the treat. She earned it! Be extra quick with your acknowledgment, because many dogs will take a step or two toward the treat. Ideally, you want to prevent your dog from getting into this habit now.

5. Of course, you don't have to always ask for these four skills at the same time or in this particular order. Mix it up and keep your dog guessing! I find this to be a great way to keep things exciting and engaging for you and your dog. Also, if your dog is wound up and has a lot of energy, focus on keeping your timing extra tight, as the moments of success come rapidly. If you miss acknowledging those moments, you are also missing opportunities to communicate to your dog that you wish to see these skills repeated.

6. Once your dog is confidently sitting, lying down, and so on you can evolve your lure into hand signals that resemble the original lure at first, and gradually turn them into whichever hand signals feel comfortable. The easiest way to get traction on this process is to fake your dog out a bit and make her think that you are luring with a treat while you actually have the treat in your other hand or somewhere nearby. Now say the words and use the hand motion just *before* she gets into a particular position and then once she does, give her the treat from the opposite hand. This will convey that you want your dog looking at your hand for the signal, not the treat.

Come

This is another critical skill that all dogs need to learn. The last thing you want is your dog running into harm's way only to ignore you when you call her back to you. Make it a big priority to teach "come" as soon as possible. Here's what to do:

1. Starting in a quiet, familiar environment, have your dog between you and, if possible, another person. If you're teaching "come" by yourself, keep your dog on a long lead leash. At first, make sure your dog is only a few feet from you. Remember, the closer you are to your dog, the easier it is for her to learn initially. Show your dog that you have a reward in hand and then call her to you in a really inviting and possibly a high-pitched voice. Forget about your dignity! Just focus on being exciting to your dog. The goal is not just to get your dog to come to you, but to make her really *want* to come to you. When she takes even one step toward you, praise her enthusiastically, and say "Great, come!" Give her the reward. Again, the key here is to make your dog realize that by coming to you, good things are going to happen for her. If you're working with another person, have them repeat the same drill so that your dog is running back and forth between the two of you.

2. Gradually increase the distance from which you ask your dog to come. If at any time during training your dog stops coming to you, reduce the distance and very slowly try to work back to that point. Keep in mind that moderate- to high-energy dogs usually respond to "come" during controlled training sessions very well, whereas a more reserved dog may need a minute to process what's going on. Either way, practice this randomly and often when your dog doesn't expect it, such as while you're cooking or working on your computer. This is how you'll begin to help her generalize the concept outside of the initial training sessions.

3. Once you've succeeded repeatedly at home, take your training sessions outside. Keep your dog on a long lead leash so that you

ultimately have control. A surefire way to get most dogs to come is to run away from them. Most dogs love to play chase, so make yours chase you! When she catches you, say "Yes, come!" and give her a reward.

4. Over the next several months of training, prioritize taking your dog to lots of different places and practicing "come." I can't emphasize this too much, as this is how you'll teach your dog to generalize this skill in various environments. Just make sure to have your dog on a long lead leash.

Stay

Teaching "stay" can be broken down into three major categories: stay for a period of time, stay with distance, and most important, stay while distracted. The key is to break this down and add only one new variable at a time so you don't overwhelm your dog. Here's what to do:

STAY FOR A PERIOD OF TIME

1. Remain close to your dog during this process. Ask her to sit or lie down, and reward her so she gets excited to start the training session. As soon as she sits or lies down, put your palm facing her as though you're telling her to stop. Be really obvious with your hand signal. Find the tiniest reason to acknowledge a stay at this point. So if she doesn't move, even for a split second, say "Great, stay!" and give her a treat. If she does move, calmly say "No" and try again.

2. Once you've mastered a brief stay for a few seconds, gradually add time to your stay. Start with one second, then two, then three. Work up to thirty seconds. If your dog is a hyper, high-energy dog, then know that "stay" can be a monumental accomplishment for her, so focus on rewarding smaller moments more frequently at first. If your dog is lower energy, you might be able to add time to the stay sooner than expected. You can mix up the time periods you ask for along the way to avoid being too predictable. When you're ready to release your dog from a stay,

say something like "Okay" or "Release" or whatever word or phrase you choose to let your dog know the stay is over. If your dog breaks her stay at any point, say "No," withhold the reward, and try the drill again for a shorter period of time.

STAY WITH DISTANCE

1. Starting just a few inches from your dog, ask for a basic stay. If you are on the ground and your dog is particularly clingy, as many puppies are, begin by moving just your head a few inches away. If your dog holds her stay, reward for the minor progress. Work up to being able to stand up as she holds her stay. Again, reward her.

2. Now add distance. Take a quarter of a step backward and return *promptly* to your dog and reward before she has a chance to move. Notice that you're not pausing at the end of your stay yet. Most people intuitively do this, and it can delay your progress. Remember, *change one variable at a time*. In this case the variable is moving away, not moving away, and also pausing.

3. Move backward one step, then two, then three. Slowly work your way up to greater distances. The one constant here is that you immediately return to your dog and reward her before she breaks out of the stay once you've reached your desired distance. If your dog fails two times in a row, you are asking too much of her too early, so decrease the distance the next two or three times. Do not rush this process! For some dogs, you may need a few training sessions to work up to five feet; others may achieve fifty feet during the first training session.

4. Once your dog is staying at a distance for twenty to thirty times in a row, then work on adding more time at various distances. This is when you begin pausing. This is a really magical moment, because you are now combining duration and distance in a single exercise. At first, be content with a one- or two-second stay with some distance. Work your way up to thirty seconds over the next week or so.

▶ STAY WHILE DISTRACTED

Teaching your dog to stay at doorways is a great way to introduce this concept. You have the advantage of being able to work in a familiar environment (your home) with a more distracting environment at a near distance (the outside). Always prioritize your dog's safety above everything else—practice this with a leash on if there's a street in front of your door, or introduce the concept to a fenced-in backyard. Here's what to do:

1. Ask your dog to "sit" by the door and then "stay." Since an open door is a fairly significant distraction by itself, we are going to start small. Most dogs understand that when your hand goes near the doorknob, something exciting is about to happen. Touch the doorknob. If your dog doesn't budge, reward her. This is a great example of being one step ahead of your dog, something all good dog trainers are good at. You've rewarded your dog before she even had a chance to break her stay. Repeat this several times.

2. Now take a more significant, but still fairly easy step: Open the door an inch or two and then close it. Again, if your dog holds that stay, give a treat and authentic praise! Gradually open the door farther until it's wide open. Have your dog stay for a few seconds and encourage her to look at you. (Now your "leave it/ watch me" combo training is going to pay off!) After doing this several times, you should notice that your dog automatically begins to anticipate that you want her to look at you and does so. Give her an extra big reward for such an accomplishment—this is called a "jackpot reward."

3. If at any point your dog breaks her stay, you should simply say "No" and close the door. Limiting access to the place your dog wants to go—in this case, outside—is the consequence for breaking stay. You should also withhold the reward. It is critical to practice this independently of when you are actually opening the door in real life—for example, when guests arrive or when you arrive home with your arms filled with groceries. That's because you'll likely not be able to focus to appropriately teach your dog. Dogs do not respond well to a distracted teacher.

4. Provided your dog is doing well so far, now make the outside really exciting. Ask your dog to "stay." Throw a fun toy or even a treat out the door. If your dog resists the urge to cross the threshold, celebrate with her! You may have to cut back on the length of the stay, since you've added a new variable here, but you can eventually work up to longer periods of time. Reward for the smallest increments of success here.

5. For the next year, I strongly recommend insisting that your dog hold a sit/stay for five to ten seconds at every open door leading to outside before allowing her to walk through it. Be really consistent. This is a biggie!

▶ Teaching All Skills from a Distance

Dogs are super-sensitive to distance. Your dog may listen when you're up close, but as you move farther away and stretch the training bubble—the distance between your eyes and your dog's eyes—it can get more difficult. There's a definite learning curve to this. You've already learned how to teach "stay from a distance," a prerequisite before your dog can learn other skills from a distance. Once your dog knows that, you can apply the same concepts with other skills. Here's what to do:

1. Let's take "sit," for example. Ask your dog to sit while you're just a few inches away from her. If you have success, you may try it from a little farther. If not, say "No," withhold the reward, and get closer to get a successful "sit." Reward when she complies and then work up to a slightly greater distance. Gradually increase the distance even more. At first, progress is very small and incremental; you'll notice that your dog is compliant only up to a certain specific point. This is normal. Your dog may need some extra time to process this new concept, so be patient.

2. Next, try more difficult skills, such as "leave it," following the basic formula I've explained. Your goal will always be to find that point when your dog goes from listening to you to not

listening to you. Trust me, with a little experimentation you'll be able to find that *exact point*. This is where you need to concentrate your efforts, so you can move on from that spot very slowly and deliberately.

3. As your dog gets better at this, take your training outside. Of course, when you do, always keep your dog on a long lead leash to be certain she stays safe. Also, remember to take a step back in training because you've changed a major variable: the environment.

Teaching All Skills with Distractions

Your dog may listen to everything you say when you're home and perform any action you ask for, but the real trick is getting her to do that any place, any time. We've already covered staying while distracted, the prerequisite to training your dog to do all of the things I teach in this book while distracted. However, don't wait for real-world situations—any attempts to teach your dog while she's, say, in the process of lunging for a cat or excitedly sniffing around a new environment will prove futile most of the time because she'll be too excited to learn a new concept.

Instead, set up training exercises to prepare your dog for these inevitable situations. That way she'll have a foundation when presented with distractions in real life. For the first six months to a year, play it safe and do this training with a leash on, even for those dogs who won't leave your side. Also, it will likely help your dog focus if you exercise her before distraction training. Lastly, know that moderate- to high-energy dogs are more likely to be distracted at first since they are typically more curious about things in general; lower-energy dogs aren't usually captivated by distractions as much, so you might expect success with this skill even sooner. Either way, here's what to do:

1. Begin just outside of your house, maybe in your driveway or yard. Warm your dog up with the "leave it/look at me" combo exercise we went over earlier. Getting your dog's eyes on you even when there are distractions is crucial to success. If your

dog cannot do this in a particular environment using her favorite currency, you are not ready to move on yet.

2. Next, try going to a new environment, ideally one with some distractions (but not too many at first), such as a friend's house or a park during off-hours. *If you want your dog to listen to you around distractions, in a variety of settings, you need to practice often in these places and around unfamiliar distractions.* Keeping her on a long lead leash, ask your pet to do the basics such as "sit," "come," and especially the "leave it/look at me" combo. Do your absolute best to be upbeat and engaging as you work with your dog, as though you're saying to her, "Hey, forget all that other stuff you're looking at. The interesting stuff is over *here*."

3. If your dog is so distracted that all attempts to get her attention on you fail, this likely means the distraction is too great and you should take a step back in your training. Do that by creating distance between the distraction and your dog until you can get her eyes back on you using her favorite currency. In some instances, you may even need to make sure the distraction is completely out of sight. This brings up a critical point: you must become very good at assessing when your dog is in a teachable mind-set at a given time. If she won't even sit for you or look at you, this probably means she's not yet prepared for the situation you've put her in.

4. When you are ready for the next step, try a more distracting environment such as the outside perimeter of a dog park. Reward heavily each time your dog focuses on you and not the other dogs she sees. Ask her to "sit," "lie down," and "stay," for instance, and then give her heartfelt praise and a reward. I know that when it comes to training you may well quickly wean off treats when working on some easy, basic skills such as "sit." However, in this situation the reward isn't for the fact that she's sitting but because she's staying focused in the face of distractions. While you're distraction training, reward extra generously for an extended period of time, even several months.

▶ Leash Training

What I love about leash training is that it's a great time to start combining many of the things we've taught in this chapter, such as the "leave it/watch me" combo and "stay" with distractions. Leash walking typically takes three weeks to six months for your dog to master, depending on how consistent you are and how energetic your dog is. It's certainly not as simple as "sit" and "stay." It takes a lot of work! While some dogs have a nice slow walk, many others need more help in that department. In most cases, by asking your dog to walk slowly, you are asking her to do something that is highly unnatural. Please be empathetic to this point! Humans are relatively slow-moving mammals compared to those of the four-legged variety.

Remember, don't attempt leash training during regularly scheduled walks or housetraining sessions. Keep them separate. Also, I know I may sound like a broken record here, but I can't stress enough how important it is that you meet your pet's physical and mental needs just *prior* to leash walking training. Dogs cannot absorb intricate concepts like walking extra slowly next to a person—nor is it reasonable to expect them to—until you can get their overflowing energy out of them first with a game of fetch or other activity. Here's what to do:

1. As with all new concepts, introduce this one in a very familiar environment such as inside your house. As you begin to walk with your dog on leash, stop immediately if you think your dog is about to start speeding up and pulling. *Remember, the best time to address unwanted behaviors is before they occur.* Start walking in the complete opposite direction, asking your dog to look at you (you may even want to walk backward at first to emphasize this eye contact).

2. Throughout the lesson, ask your dog to look at you repeatedly, rewarding her each time. (While you won't require your dog to constantly stare at you while on leash, you just want to confirm that she does look at you reliably when you ask her to do so in this setting before moving on.) Ask her to do easy things like "sit" a few times, just to keep her enthusiastic about the training session. Of course, you should also reward for these easy things

since you are now asking your dog to do them with a major variable change—the leash! Your main priority throughout leash training is to have longer periods of time without tension on the leash. Repeat this drill indoors until your dog is walking consistently without pulling.

3. ▶ Next, take your dog outside, but stay close to home. Walking up and down your street may be best. Remember, you'll have to slow down your training here a bit, since you're adding distractions. In this case, the distraction is simply being outside. Be empathetic—give your dog a grace period at first and let her sniff around and take in the world. As you walk, reward heavily whenever there's no tension on the leash and say something like "You rock! Good dog." Remember, a reward doesn't have to be a treat: I once worked with a super-high-drive German Shepherd named Zeus, who learned how to walk on a leash very well when I used tug-of-war as the reward exclusively. He was so high-energy that when I initiated the game, he was 100 percent focused on me and not the other distractions nearby. That was one of my favorite leash walking training sessions of all time!

4. Any time your dog starts to pull forward at all or even seems like she's going to do so, stop in your tracks. Say "No" to communicate, "The pulling is the thing resulting in this next action," and then abruptly change directions. Get your dog's attention back on you by becoming super-animated or placing a treat at her nose and asking her to look at you. Eventually, you'll notice that every once in a while, your dog will begin glancing at you without your having to ask. These are really special moments, and you need to find ways to communicate how much you love it when your dog voluntarily does this. Jackpot rewards work great!

5. Teaching your dog to listen with distractions during leash training is similar to what we covered earlier in the distraction training section, but now you'll be doing it while moving. When

you encounter a distraction on a walk, it's important to test for teachability. You do this by asking your dog to "sit" periodically as you get farther and farther away from the distraction. When she sits, you are likely in teachable territory. The goal now is to get her eyes on you and advance very slowly, using rewards liberally, and taking steps back when necessary. You may need to back off from the distraction at about ten feet or even a block and, with more severe cases, you may need to go out of sight and work up to very distracting scenarios. If your dog absolutely will not look at you or sit, you are in unteachable territory. Chances are your dog is just not ready for this situation. Don't become frustrated! You just need to gradually work up to it over time.

Head Collars

If your dog is literally too strong for you and you cannot control your dog, a head collar may help. A head collar goes around your dog's snout and acts much like a halter for a horse. If your dog attempts to pull, her head rises or goes to one side or another, so it makes walking fast impractical. Some people might confuse these collars' appearance with a muzzle, but they do not prevent barking or biting. These collars are humane, whereas prong, electric, or choke collars are certainly not.

Head collars are a shortcut to leash training, but they will not teach your dog to walk nicely. Since this is outside-in training, the moment the head collar comes off your dog will probably go right back to pulling. That's why I don't recommend head collars unless you really need to use them. If you do, introduce a head collar slowly; most dogs need time to adjust, since the collar can be a bit awkward at first. Most dogs learn to tolerate them within a couple of weeks or so.

▶ Teaching Your Dog Proper Greetings (No Jumping!)

Many people like when their dogs run to them and jump all over them whenever they come home. However, you may not want your dog to do that—especially if you have guests over or if you have a rather large dog who can literally knock you over. Personally, I love it when my dogs jump on me if I ask them to! The key part of that sentence is that I'm *asking* them to greet me that way; otherwise, they won't do it without permission.

By nature, jumping is usually a very friendly behavior—dogs simply are psyched to see us. However, it's important to teach your dog proper greetings. Then you can pick and choose if and when she can let loose and show her excitement by jumping. Before starting this lesson, if you notice your dog is in a super-animated mood and unable to process what you're teaching, you need to first let her burn off some energy with a little exercise. Here's what to do:

1. Work on teaching your dog proper greetings in your house—at first, when no one else is around. As you approach your dog slowly, if she jumps up for even a second or indicates she's about to, say "No" in a quiet voice and take a step back abruptly. In this case, the consequence is stepping back so your dog can't physically interact with you, as well as no reward. She must have all paws on the ground to get any attention from you! However, if she hesitates for even a split second and doesn't jump, praise her and reward her. The idea is that she'll start realizing that she'll get what she wants—your attention and a reward—when she doesn't jump.

2. Next, set up more challenging training sessions. Have a partner squeak a toy, for instance, or even have your friends encourage your dog to jump on them. There is a lot of value in setting up super-tempting exercises like this because ultimately your dog should listen to you above everyone else. At this point in training, she shouldn't be allowed to jump on guests, even if they say, "Oh, no worries. It's fine," as many guests will. Again, the point is that you and only you can say whether or not the jumping is okay. Otherwise, your dog must keep all four paws on the ground until you give permission.

3. Any time you anticipate that your dog is about to jump, such as when you first come home, at first take a deep breath, put down your belongings, and walk past the bundle of energy that is your

dog toward your treats (you may want to keep soft treats handy by the front door). Then ask your dog to "sit" and "stay." Reward heavily when she does so, but be a bit more reserved than usual, so as not to encourage hyper behavior. Over the next three weeks or so, insist on longer increments of time.

4. A common mistake people make, particularly when their dog jumps on guests, is expecting the guest to do the steps I've advised you to do in this section. *You* are the one who needs to teach your dog how to act appropriately. It's also a good idea to have your dog on leash when company is over so that you have extra control of your dog. (And, again, if you know that you are going to have company over and your dog is on a full battery, get her outside to burn off some energy just prior to your guests arriving. By your doing this, she'll calm down and may not even jump at all. She'll also quickly learn that she gets to hang out with you guys when she chills out.)

You will not be able to teach your dog not to jump on guests if your attention is divided. So instead of trying to entertain your guest and train your dog simultaneously, tell the visitor, "Excuse me, I need to spend the next sixty seconds teaching my dog to not jump." Then ask your dog to "sit" and "stay." Once she complies, allow your guest to pet her. If your dog shows she's even *thinking* about jumping, create a human barrier between her and the person and, again, ask for a "sit" and "stay."

Another option: If your dog is really hyper or unexercised, or you just don't want to devote much attention to training at the moment your guests arrive, remove your dog from the setting. For example, you may want to keep her in the bedroom when your visitors first enter your home and then, once they are settled, you can try bringing her out on leash so you can teach with more focus and attention.

ASK *Zak*

Hiring a Trainer

"I think I need some extra help with training. What are my options?"

Working with a dog trainer can be a great way to speed along training or to help you work through a particular behavioral issue with your pet. However, you have to choose wisely. Dog training is an unregulated industry. Anyone without any qualifications whatsoever can call themselves a dog trainer. And believe me, they do! This obviously leads to a lot of bad options out there.

It's important to find an authentic positive trainer. Almost all dog trainers claim to be positive trainers, but most of them are not. Their general game plan may be to pay lip service to positive training methods, but if they don't get instant results, they'll often view this as justification to use an overabundance of force in lieu of real teaching. No matter what your specific dog is like, force is never the answer.

So how do you avoid this kind of trainer? Ask questions like, "How do I discipline my dog when she jumps on me?" and see how they respond. If they tend to encourage thoughtful teaching and avoid telling you to knee your dog in the chest or how to manhandle your dog in some way, you're off to a good start. You can also ask, "Do I need a special collar?"—another great question to separate the bad apples from the good ones. If they tell you that you need a prong, choke, metal, or electric collar, they are not the trainer for you. These guys will almost always tell you that these collars are fine as long as you use them properly. However, there is absolutely no proper way to use these devices. Also, if a trainer uses the common buzzwords "alpha," "dominant," or "balanced" (which means they likely rely on physical corrections), cross them off your list. *You don't need to pay someone to tell you to constantly punish your dog in the name of teaching.*

Instead, seek a trainer who is well versed in the latest science and ethics in dog training. For example, many trainers who use clickers have a clue about ethical training because clicker training is specifically designed to acknowledge the positive things dogs do (even if you don't want to use a clicker, you can still hire these trainers). Also, most knowledgeable trainers will ask you a lot of questions so that they can best understand why your dog is behaving in a particular way, rather than simply attributing her behaviors to some superstition or breed stereotype. Here's an overview of the various training options:

Group Classes: I'm a huge fan of group classes for many reasons. First of all, many cover all the basics that you might need to know. Also, such classes are excellent for socialization, provided the instructor makes an effort to keep dogs with behavioral issues at a distance. Plus, this option is typically a lot less expensive than private lessons. Check out your local pet supply store or local Humane Society for options in your area and ask your vet for suggestions. But again, beware of old-school trainers here. They're everywhere!

Private Lessons: Private lessons can be great for people who need a little extra help with their dog. If you follow all of my advice in this book and still have issues with, say, chewing or jumping or housetraining, then a private instructor can address your very specific situation. The same is true if your dog has severe separation issues, aggression, or other anxieties. The Association of Professional Dog Trainers can help you find a trainer in your area. Again, you can also ask your veterinarian, local Humane Society, and friends who have dogs for recommendations. Make sure you ask the questions I mentioned earlier, and always ask for references.

Day Training/Board and Train: I strongly advise that you *don't* consider this option, where you drop your dog off for the day or even for weeks at time at a training facility, and they promise they'll train your dog. It can be very pricey, and because your dog is out of sight, you won't really know what methods the trainer is using. Most important, I know that my job as a trainer isn't to train your dog for you—it's to show *you* how to do that. Remember, the most crucial factor when teaching your dog is developing the bond between the both of you. Another trainer can't do that for you. In short, these board-and-train options take the most important person—you!—out of the equation. I see no point in that.

Logistics of Training

"How many times should I train my dog each day, and how long should each session last?"

When introducing new concepts during your primary training sessions, you should be in a familiar environment such as inside your house. In general, one hour of formal training per day, split up into three to six training sessions, is best. But that's not all! You have the rest of the day to do more casual (or secondary) training in real-world situations. Maybe you're watching TV and a dog walks past your house, but your dog doesn't bark. Acknowledge and reward this! Or maybe you see that your dog is about to steal food off of the counter. Get over there fast and create a barrier with your hand and turn this into a brief "leave it" training session.

Also, remember that once your dog understands the various concepts you are teaching, it's time to move to a slightly more distracting setting. But don't go crazy here. Sometimes we have the tendency to take steps that are too big. Always break things down, one step at a time. Also, practice everywhere you can—the park, your pet supply store, in your neighborhood, and anywhere else you want your dog to listen.

Consistency

"My dog knows the basic commands, but she seems to pick and choose when she listens to me. Why isn't she consistent?"

I get this question a lot. Why? Because most people have the expectation that their dogs should make faster progress than they do, particularly in unfamiliar environments. Also, they may be using an inadequate currency, cutting out rewards too early, or they are changing up multiple variables simultaneously. Remember, you've got to practice every skill in many different settings and under different circumstances for your dog to fully get it. Most important, don't underestimate the importance of time and patience.

Too Many Treats

"I'm afraid that if I give my dog a treat every time she does something I like, she'll quickly become overweight. Should I be worried?"

First of all, since you're using treats like chicken and you're keeping those pieces very small (remember, the size of a pea for a medium to large dog and the size of a grain of rice for a small dog), there should be no real likelihood of your dog gaining weight. If your dog is putting on too much weight, that's a sign you should make your treats even smaller or reduce her overall food intake per your vet's recommendations.

Also, as I explained earlier, eventually, over time, you can phase out treats. They are not a permanent part of training—unless you want them to be. Of course, don't forget about the power of play. Far too many people insist on using food rewards with a dog who would be just as happy, if not happier, if they would use play as the reward. Plus, such exercise encourages fitness and weight loss!

CHAPTER SEVEN

HOW TO TROUBLESHOOT THE MOST COMMON BEHAVIOR PROBLEMS: BARKING, CHEWING, LEASH PULLING, PUPPY BITING, AGGRESSION, JUMPING UP, AND MORE

Your dog may be the love of your life, but that doesn't mean he's always going to behave as you wish. His actions can certainly test your patience. My coauthor, Dina, knows this all too well. She adopted her second dog, Brody, from a shelter when he was four months old. He was so affectionate that he'd literally sprint across the house and leap into her lap to smother her with kisses. She said she thought that he'd never do anything to upset her. But then he started chewing everything in sight—socks, pen caps, her bedroom armoire. He'd grab onto the toilet paper roll, pull it about six feet, and then shred as much of it as he could before she could stop him. Dina said that when her kids used the excuse, "My dog ate my homework," they were actually telling the truth. She was at her wit's end.

Having worked with thousands of dogs in the past decade, I hear the same sort of complaints repeatedly from my clients. They tell me, "My dog is always barking!" or "He's destroying everything in my house!" Trust me, there's not much I haven't dealt with.

In this chapter, I'll address the most common questions I've heard throughout my years of training. For each, I'll give you a glimpse into *why* your dog might be misbehaving, which is what you must first understand before you can effectively resolve any of these problems. (Addressing the symptoms but not the cause by, say, using a bitter-tasting spray in the case of chewing or a prong collar when your dog pulls on a walk will *not* give you real results.) Then I'll give you the formula for handling such behaviors by showing you how to teach your dog to follow your guidance.

Before we get into the actual behavioral problems themselves, I want to remind you of a few big-picture points that will keep you on track. *Remember the following as you address the issues individually*:

- As always, consistency is key. For instance, if you don't want your dog barking when the doorbell rings, but you sometimes let him do it just for the heck of it, you are not being very clear with your communication.

- Control your dog's surroundings for the first year of training—even longer if you're experiencing behavioral problems. If you always supervise your dog or make sure he's in a contained area when you can't watch him, he can't sneak off to do something you don't want him to do. This way, the unwanted habit is either stopped or not established in the first place.

- If your dog isn't acting as you want, then that's on you, not him. He just hasn't fully learned what you expect of him. Dogs have a lot to take in when learning our expectations and way of communicating. Please be empathetic.

- If your dog shows the slightest sign that he doesn't really understand how you want him to behave—usually when he does something you don't like two or more times in a row—take a step back in training. This is particularly true when you change a variable on him, such as his surroundings.

- Finally, know this: *About 90 percent of unwanted behaviors happen because your dog is simply bored.* That's why they are common with higher-energy dogs. If a dog isn't being stimulated both mentally and physically, he'll use that pent-up energy some other way—for instance, he might dig up your yard or chew the pillows on your couch. In fact, researchers at Bristol University surveyed four thousand people with dogs and found that, on average, the less a person played with their pet, the more behavioral problems the dog had.[1] For many pet parents, making sure their dogs get adequate exercise will be a lifelong commitment, as it is the most practical, natural way to address most chronic, unwanted behaviors.

LEASH PULLING

Why dogs do this: Dogs pull on a leash because they walk faster than we do or because they're very interested in sniffing and investigating something out of their reach. Plain and simple. Remember, many of the dogs who were bred for all-day stamina and endurance are the same ones we're now asking to walk slowly on a leash next to us. Some were selectively bred to be good hunting dogs who would make a beeline, without hesitation, at full speed to retrieve the kill. I just want you to understand that when attempting to teach your dog this skill, you're fighting the very same qualities humans purposely selected for over thousands of years! However, keep in mind that the ultimate trait we've selected for when creating dogs was their ability to take direction from people. This trumps all else. In other words, the good news is that dogs are primed to learn from humans, so with a little patience yours *will* eventually understand the foreign concept of walking slowly.

How to handle the behavior: First, take a few steps back and reprioritize leash training as I fully outlined on page 135, chapter 6. Your dog may just need a refresher course, especially on the "leave it/ watch me" combo, which needs to be solid for leash walking. Also, know that you are most likely not meeting your pet's physical and mental needs *prior* to leash walking training. Dogs cannot absorb intricate concepts like walking extra slowly next to you until you can get their overflowing energy burned off first with a game of fetch or other activity. If you don't do that, then know that you'll have to be tolerant of the pulling until you've walked long enough for him to fatigue a bit.

Along with their dog's pulling on a leash, some of my clients ask about a concept called leash reactivity. That's when your dog is on leash and barks and lunges at other dogs or people in a manner that can be perceived as threatening. This is different from a dog who barks excitedly or out of frustration because he wants to play. It's a more stressful response. What's interesting is that some dogs interact perfectly well with other dogs when off leash but show such seemingly aggressive behavior while on leash. "The restriction of the leash prevents their being able to approach and retreat freely, sometimes leading them to possibly feel trapped and to use reactive behavior to keep themselves safe," explains Meghan Herron, DVM, DACVB, director of the Behavioral Medicine Clinic at The Ohio State University College of Veterinary Medicine.

If your dog is experiencing leash reactivity, practice the leash walking with distractions steps that I outlined on page 136, chapter 6, in less stimulating settings, perhaps in front of your house where you can easily get back home if need be.

In some cases, severe leash reactivity may take a while to overcome and will require you to help your dog become desensitized to whatever is causing him to react.

SEPARATION ANXIETY

▶ **Why dogs do this:** Separation anxiety affects many dogs to varying degrees. Keep in mind that there's a difference between a puppy barking for attention frequently during his first few weeks and significant, sustained separation anxiety. Problematic separation anxiety is exhibited when dogs become distressed when they're left alone. Dogs experiencing it will usually follow you everywhere and will begin whining or frantically barking when you're out of sight. They may drool and pant, and they also may attempt to break out of the area they're being contained in (even if doing so causes physical harm to them), have more potty accidents than usual, and destroy property by digging or chewing, even *after* you've adequately exercised them.

How to handle the behavior: Don't expect to resolve this issue quickly—it can take some time, depending on the severity of the case. For the most part, you won't be able to fully cure your dog's anxiety, but you can help mitigate it. If your dog is experiencing significant distress, consult with your vet right away. Here are some other things you can do:

- Just as with humans, regular physical and mental exercise helps tremendously at reducing almost all types of anxiety in dogs. If possible, exercise your dog right before you leave the house.

- Having your dog relax in another room in his crate or puppy-proofed area while you are, say, cooking dinner can be a good way to introduce the concept of being away from you. Start with a few minutes and gradually work up to longer periods of time.

- Make sure your departures are very low-key. Get in the habit of situating your dog in a bedroom or other area that he is comfortable in so that he can't easily observe you going through your routine of getting your keys, putting on your shoes, and so on. That may help prevent him from becoming overly anxious.

- Giving your dog something to do while you are gone may help, too. For example, there are toys designed to hold treats that come out as your dog paws or chews at the toy. This can provide a good distraction.

- Remember that yelling at your dog or punishing him for destroying property, having potty accidents, or barking because he's anxious will likely make matters worse. Just don't do this—ever.

- When it comes to anxiety, many pet parents jump to medication too easily. I'm not a huge fan of medicating dogs in lieu of teaching them, but if your dog is harming himself or seems overly anxious, talk to your vet about whether or not this might be appropriate for your dog.

JUMPING UP

Why dogs do this: For most dogs, jumping on people comes very naturally. They do it primarily because they want to interact with you near your face. However, since humans are taller than dogs, they have to jump up to reach. I promise you this: dogs do *not* jump on people because they're trying to dominate us, as many traditional trainers may tell you. Your dog jumps because he's just really excited to see you or the people who visit your home, and you haven't yet taught him to behave otherwise. Also, mellow dogs rarely have a problem with excessive unwanted jumping—it's the high-energy ones who are more likely to find it really difficult to keep all four paws on the ground. You may just need some extra persistence with them here.

How to handle the behavior: This is such a common issue, so I teach proper greetings as part of basic training (see page 137, chapter 6). If your dog is jumping, then go back to that chapter and reteach this important skill.

CHEWING

▶ **Why dogs do this:** Puppies chew because they're teething; it hurts as their teeth come in (just as this process does for human babies) and gnawing on things helps relieve that pain. Older dogs may chew for various reasons: either it has become a bad habit because they were never taught as puppies the proper things to chew on, or they're bored so they resort to chewing to occupy themselves. Also, remember that dogs love exploring their environment. "The sense of taste and feeling in the mouth is the first sense to develop (dogs are born blind and deaf!) so it's understandable that young puppies use their mouth to check things out," says Dr. Herron. Chewing is also instinctual—thousands of years ago, dogs had to chew and grind through bone and marrow to survive; many still have that innate desire.[2]

Regardless of the reason, rest assured that a dog can learn to stop chewing at any age. One caveat: Some dogs may chew because they're scared or anxious. If you think that's the case, then you'll have to address those causes specifically if you want the chewing to stop. Of course, if your dog is potentially harming himself by chewing dangerous substances, talk to your vet.

How to handle the behavior: First, remember that your dog cannot chew up your couch or sneak off to tear apart your favorite shoes if you're supervising him or otherwise containing him. So go back to the basics and completely control his surroundings, even if he's five years old. That's paramount if you want to put an end to this problem.

Also, understand that in many cases you actually shouldn't prevent your dog from chewing, especially if he's teething. Instead, the key is to teach him what he *can* chew on. Leave a variety of bones, antlers, and other durable and safe toys of various textures around the house. You may have to experiment a bit to find out what your dog likes.

Assuming that you are supervising your dog, if you notice him wandering over to your shoe and gnawing on it, then do what it takes to get his attention on you. This might mean clapping your hands or getting super-animated to distract him momentarily from the chewing. Avoid grabbing him or the shoe at this point, as you want *him* to originate restraint (remember, inside out!). Once you've got his attention, give him a sincere "Yes!" and a chew toy of comparable texture to satisfy him. Even have a brief play session with the toy. Now you've expressed two things to your dog: "I've got something that you're allowed to chew on over here, and listening to me makes your life fun and interesting." Next time, keep your shoes (or any other object your dog might destroy) out of reach.

Lastly, make sure your dog is getting plenty of playtime with you. That way, maybe the next time he has some downtime, he'll take a nap or just feel content instead of chewing apart every object he finds! Gimmicks such as sprays designed to deter chewing are an attempt to squelch the behavior instead of addressing the causes head-on. Teach your dog to understand you and think for himself, not to just avoid the items because of a bad-tasting spray.

PUPPY BITING

Why dogs do this: Puppy biting, also referred to as mouthing, is the number one thing I'm asked about. Even if you follow every bit of advice I'm about to give you, a puppy will still be a little biting machine for many weeks, starting at about eight weeks old. This is completely normal. Whereas puppies chew because they're teething, they bite because they want to engage you but don't understand that you don't play that way. If your puppy did not get the benefit of being with his mother and siblings until at least eight weeks of age, you may need to do a bit more work to help him learn how to appropriately play and use his mouth when interacting with people and other dogs. "A puppy's mother and litter mates typically teach a puppy how to control his biting by letting him know when he is biting too hard or too much," explains Dr. Herron. This is a concept known as "bite inhibition."

How to handle the behavior: Be one step ahead of your puppy. Since you know your puppy is likely to bite you when you interact with him at all, come armed with a small treat. Let your dog know you have a treat by letting him smell it and then ask him to "sit." Reward him for the sit. This is the first step to showing him the behavior you want when you approach. As you see, we are not waiting for the biting to occur to then correct it. This method is much more powerful, because the best time to address unwanted behaviors is *before* they occur— something you'll become a lot better at detecting as you get to know your dog. Of course, you'll have to do this consistently for several days to a few weeks until your dog starts to get that the right way to interact with you is by first sitting calmly, not attacking you with his little piranha-like mouth!

What about when you go to pick him up and he starts chomping with those puppy teeth? Again, grab a treat and distract him from your flesh or clothes with it, but instead of immediately giving it to him, allow him to lick your fingers and the treat while you hold it firmly. When dogs are in "food mode," their mouths become less about wanting to grab and play and more about tasting and eating. Basically *any time your dog begins to lick where he would otherwise bite, you're on the right track*. Do your best to avoid just giving your dog the treat all at once; instead do so little by little.

Of course, there will still be times when your dog won't be able to resist biting. The key in those cases is to teach your dog that it's okay if he bites stuff, but only if he bites things you approve of, such as a rope toy or a stuffed animal. I do this by teaching a proper game of puppy tug-of-war in a dedicated training session. Here's how: As you approach your puppy, knowing that he's likely to bite, bring his attention to the toy and make it exciting. Move it around on the ground toward and away from your dog. If he pounces on it and tries to get it, you've got him right where you want him. Once he grabs it, pull back just enough to where he still feels like he has some control of the toy. Let him do this for several seconds. When you've decided you want him to let go, avoid prying it from his mouth. Instead, make the toy completely immobile as though it's attached to a tree. Wait up to two minutes. When your puppy lets go (and he eventually will, as long as you act like you don't care if he does), say "Yep, let go!" and promptly give the toy back, to remind him that playing by your rules results in a fun game he gets to play with you. You'll likely notice very fast progress on this—in as little as one training session—and your puppy should soon be letting go when you ask within seconds instead of minutes.

What do you do when you *do* get chomped on by your puppy? First, though I understand that this kind of pain can make any person instantly upset, it's critical to keep your cool. Then you have three major options, depending on your desire or ability to train at that moment:

1. Play tug-of-war as I just outlined.

2. Get your treats and do a basic training session. The goal here is to say to your dog, "Okay, I'll interact with you, but we need to do it on my terms."

3. If you can't teach at that moment or if your dog is in such an energetic state that he's unresponsive to training, say "No" in a monotone voice and put your dog in a puppy-proofed area for two to ten minutes. Many puppies will calm down and snap out of their biting mind-set after a brief time-out. If that doesn't offer some relief, a long walk should.

NIPPING

Why dogs do this: When dogs play together, they use their mouths to grab, play, and get rough. However, usually when a dog does this to a human, it's often misinterpreted as aggressive "nipping" or "snapping," though it's really just his way of playing. Also, I've known countless adult dogs who "nip" as an extension of puppy biting. For example, I was working with an adult dog named Chloe on leash training, and she wanted to bite constantly—my shoes, my shorts, or anything she could get ahold of. I understood that she simply wanted to play, but a person can easily label a dog who's not been taught proper manners as an "aggressive dog" if that person doesn't know the difference.

There's another, less common type of nipping that means, "Get away from me, I don't want to be bothered," often preceded by a dog raising his lips, baring his teeth, growling, or snapping at the air. This is most common between dogs, but when I see this behavior directed toward humans, it's often when young children interact with adult dogs. Young children usually lack the experience and manners one should have when engaging a dog. For example, some kids may see a dog as a stuffed animal and plop down on his back. After enough of these experiences, many dogs might fire off a warning snap.

Snapping could also be related to fear, when a dog feels threatened or misreads a person's intentions; it isn't acceptable, but it doesn't mean that you necessarily have an aggressive dog either. Lastly, if snapping seems uncharacteristic of your dog, it could mean that he's in some type of pain or discomfort. Take him to the vet if you think this may be the case.

How to handle the behavior: If your dog is nipping as a form of play, he is simply engaging you, so you'll need to take some time to show him the right way to play with you. Again, start by teaching a proper game of tug-of-war, which helps your dog learn that there are acceptable things to bite while playing. If you're consistent with directing your dog's desire to nip onto an acceptable toy, your dog will eventually understand.

However, if your dog is nipping because he's saying "Back off," then you'll need to proceed slowly and focus on making your dog more comfortable over time in situations that tend to prompt this behavior, such as a child being too rough or a stranger coming on too strong. For starters, make sure he has the space he needs. Also, people can do things like sit on the ground at a distance and offer some good treats in an effort to get your dog to approach them rather than their approaching him. Or maybe your pet has an extra special toy that instantly gets him in a good mood. Your job is to do your best to quickly defuse his uneasy mind-set. If these steps don't help, removing him from that setting and putting him into one that's less stressful is your next step.

It's fairly simple to differentiate between play nipping and more serious nipping. Look at your dog's overall body language. Are his ears back? Is his body stiff? Are you hearing any growling or seeing any lip curls? Then he's probably not in the mood for playing with you right now. However, does he look more carefree? Does his body seem loose and playful? Is he in a play bow? If so, consider playing with him! With consistent training, combined with showing others how to interact with your dog in a way that does not push him to nip, you might resolve this.

If your dog is making any kind of contact with another being's skin with his teeth in a way that's not playful or if you're particularly uncomfortable with his behavior, refer to the sidebar on aggression on the following page for more information.

RESOURCE GUARDING

Why dogs do this: Resource guarding is second nature to many dogs. Just as young children are often possessive of their toys and do not like sharing, some dogs have a similar mind-set. For instance, they might guard their toys, sleeping area, even their humans; however, in most cases, resource guarding involves food—many dogs just feel instinctively uneasy when another being approaches them while they're eating. This behavior is common with many mammals because successful species are good at protecting their food.

How to handle the behavior: It's best to stop resource guarding before it gets more serious by dedicating several training sessions to it. Don't wait until mealtime to do this—it's easier to work on this concept when your dog isn't particularly hungry. Also, don't procrastinate! Actually, even if your dog isn't guarding his food, this exercise may help prevent him from ever doing so.

First, put a small bit of your dog's food in his bowl. Give your dog some space as he eats, but walk near him several times, dropping small bits of chicken liberally near his bowl as you pass. Do this for two to three minutes at a time over several days to weeks. The goal here is to communicate, "I'm good. I always have your best interest at heart, and you do not need to feel threatened by me." You want him to have a positive association with having a human near him during his mealtimes.

Most dogs will change their tune at this point and be a bit more polite as you approach, since it's now "raining chicken." If your dog is acting nicer, ask him to "sit," reward him when he does, and then pick up his bowl for a split second and set it down, as if to say, "I may pick this up at any time, but I may also give it right back." Reward repeatedly as you do this, and gradually increase the amount of time you hold the food bowl before giving it back. Lots of repetition can make this easier over time, though the more established this behavior is, the longer it may take to resolve. You can apply the same basic formula if your dog is possessive of his toys, too. Also, if your dog is actually snapping at you or trying to bite or attack you, other people, or animals while he eats, see the section on aggression that follows.

Aggression

It's important to understand what we mean by aggression. First, know that an energetic dog who barks a lot, nips because he's a puppy or is simply trying to play, lunges on the leash during walks, or jumps on you or guests is probably *not* a dog with a major aggression problem unless those behaviors include apparent intentional efforts to cause harm. Also, if your dog gets into an occasional scuffle, that doesn't necessarily mean he's truly aggressive.

There is no formal definition for dog aggression; however, based on my own research and experience I've come to define it as follows: when a dog deliberately growls, bites, snaps, or acts in a way meant to ensure his own perceived safety or the safety of someone or something that he values. While there are many reasons a dog might become aggressive, very often it's fear-based or related to pent-up energy and a lack of exercise. (In the case of lack of exercise, many dogs may be more likely to be "on edge" and therefore more eager to protect something they value—something a regular game of fetch or other engaging activity can help fix.) Genetics also plays a big part, though there's little to no evidence that a particular breed of dog is likely to be more aggressive than another.[3] Also, in some cases a dog may suddenly start acting aggressively because he's in pain and/or has an undiagnosed medical condition or mental illness. Talk to your vet first to rule out such a possibility. In a nutshell, however, *aggressive behavior is almost always a combination of past experiences, genetics, and context.*

You may have heard that an aggressive dog is one who's just trying to dominate another animal or a person. Throughout this book, I've made it clear that the whole concept of dog-to-human dominance is a myth, and any training methods that tell you to be the "alpha" or "pack leader" are based on a misunderstanding of how dogs relate to us. However, what about dog-to-dog dominance? The American College of Veterinary Behaviorists offers this short definition of dominance in dog behavior: "In a relationship between two dogs, the dog who more often than not controls access to valuable resources is considered to have dominance over the other dog. Dominance does *not* equal aggression. Dominance can also depend on context; one dog may be the winner in one context but not in another."[4] I agree with that, and I find it interesting that when dogs share resources, they usually aren't aggressive at all. For example, dogs who live together establish basic ground rules regarding who sleeps where, who eats where, and who possesses which toys. However, they usually don't do this by fighting. Also, their dynamic is fluid—for instance, one dog might be first to choose a place to sleep while the other will get first dibs on a particular toy.

Other people explain that dominance is not a personality trait you can assign to a dog but simply a description of the relationship between individuals. I agree with that, too. However, here's the problem with the term "dominance": every person seems to have a different definition of the word; many definitions are either too narrow or too broad to have any meaningful impact on how one should address individual situations; and some definitions are flat-out wrong. That's why I think the term is rather useless and doesn't add much value when describing dog-to-dog interactions. I never use it.

So when trying to understand and interpret a dog's aggressive behaviors, again remember this: it's all about context, genetics, and the animal's past experiences. Sometimes one dog might quarrel with another as a way to communicate how he expects the other dog to behave—he might bare his teeth or snap as a warning to indicate, say, that he's uncomfortable with a rambunctious puppy and expects a differ-ent code of conduct. Also, occasionally traditional dog-to-dog communi-cation breaks down and physical altercations happen in what seems to be one dog's attempt at trying to communicate to the other, "I want that, and I *will* get it." Yet keep in mind that just because your dog gets into one fight with another dog doesn't necessarily mean those two dogs will always fight when they're together. And it certainly doesn't justify labeling your dog as "dominant" or "aggressive."

I know it can be difficult trying to figure out whether or not your dog's behaviors are signs of true aggression or not. And while I've worked with many dogs who exhibit aggressive behaviors, I would never and could never offer across-the-board advice that applies to all or even most dogs. Aggression should always be dealt with on a case-by-case basis. If your dog is biting you, other people, or any other animals in a way that is clearly not play, or if he's exhibiting behavior such as snapping, excessive growling, or anything that makes you uneasy, seek a professional positive trainer in your area with good credentials and experience. (See page 140, chapter 6, for tips on how to find one.) You could also seek the help of a certified veterinary behaviorist with good references—one who promotes only humane, positive techniques. If you're wondering at all whether you need professional help, I would say that you probably do.

It's vital that you find an expert who does *not* use "quick fix" tools like choke chains and the other ones I've mentioned throughout this book. Remember, these tools aren't very effective in the long term, and they can make the aggression even worse (see page 74, chapter 4).

BARKING

Why dogs do this: Barking is a dog's way of communicating—it's one of the most natural things they do. Dogs bark to get attention and to show excitement, happiness, fear, anxiety, suspicion, and many other emotions. A dog might bark to alert you of someone approaching, or he might bark because he gets anxious during thunderstorms. The most common types of barking are when something outside or in the distance excites your dog, he's barking simply out of habit, or he's a high-energy dog who's bored.

How to handle the behavior: You can likely resolve barking issues within a few weeks. Other than making sure your dog gets enough exercise, here are some techniques that may help:

- Set up training exercises rather than waiting for real-life situations to emerge. First, get your dog primed by asking for some easy things like "sit" or "down." Reward generously. Next, have a friend with a dog walk back and forth in front of your house, knock on the door repeatedly, or ring the doorbell—anything that's likely to tempt your dog to bark. Reward if your dog is quiet. If this sets your dog off into a barking frenzy, take a step back; for instance, you might ask your friend to, say, knock once instead of three times or even just lightly tap the door with her finger to get some traction. Find the point of compliance from your dog and work from there.

- Aside from primary training sessions, there will be times for spontaneous secondary sessions as well (which, if your dog is a big barker, may be many times each day). Dogs often indicate that they're going to bark before they do so. You might notice that your dog's ears prick up and he starts focusing on the thing he sees or hears outside. *This* is the ideal time to train your dog, *before* he barks. First, ask him to focus on you. (One more benefit of the "leave it/ look at me" combo exercise!) Initially, it may be slow going, as your dog may seemingly think, "How could you possibly expect me to look at you when there is a dog walking in front of our house?!" However, your goal is to look for tiny hints of compliance, such as a quick glance at you. If your dog does this, then immediately acknowledge his small success with an emphatic "Yes!" and reward him.

- If you are unable to get your dog's attention on you, and he continues to bark, your next step is to get him away from the distraction altogether. This may mean escorting him to a bedroom where you can get him to focus. Once you've established success here (this could take one or more training sessions), next move to the hallway and work your way closer to the door. Never mind if the distraction outside is now gone—it's still important to follow through on this impromptu training session. Reward and communicate that you love the quiet behavior.

- Your dog may bark while you are away from the house, but of course you won't be there to train him. Make sure you exercise your dog before you leave and put him in a part of the house where he is less likely to bark, such as away from a window with a view of the sidewalk. That way he'll more likely stay on track whether you're around or not.

- Keep in mind that when it comes to barking, you don't have to be all or nothing. Some people like their dog to bark once or twice to let them know something's up outside. If that's what you prefer, simply delay getting your dog's attention on you until after, say, the first or second bark and follow the preceding advice.

STEALING

Why dogs do this: Whether your dog likes to counter surf or jump up on the kitchen table when you're not looking, he's basically of the mind-set, "That smells delicious, and I'm going to get it." Hey, it happens to the best of us. If someone leaves even the tiniest bit of chocolate unattended anywhere near me, it's gone! Sorry, but I just can't resist.

How to handle the behavior: First, make sure your dog knows a basic "leave it," which I explained on page 123, chapter 6. The key of that lesson is to teach your dog to avoid temptation. Next, you need to teach a real-life "leave it" by setting up drills that resemble situations your dog may actually encounter. For instance, put a plate of deli meat on the coffee table while you're watching TV. It's fine to let your dog know it's there. If your dog doesn't go for it, let him know you like that by saying "Yes, leave it!" and reward generously. These rewards should always come from your hand (in other words, from *you*), so don't just tell your dog to pick up the meat off the table where you originally placed it.

If your dog does reach for the meat, make sure you are one step ahead of him by putting your hand or body between your dog and the plate to instantly create a barrier in front of the food. When your dog complies by not reaching for the food any further, reward him. Doing this rather than just pulling him away shows him how to think through the process himself.

However, remember that dogs don't generalize like we do, so you'll need to set up lots of different situations where you mix up variables for several weeks. For instance, leave the garbage pail open a crack or position food on the kitchen table so your dog can reach it either by jumping on a chair or pulling it down to the floor. Obviously, make sure you are supervising in these situations so that you can preempt your dog by saying "No" and creating a barrier between him and the food when he moves toward it. (Or, better yet, you can say "Yes!" and reward him when he shows restraint.) Be consistent with this as long as necessary. When your dog makes fewer attempts to get the food, then you'll know you're on the right track. Also, stealing doesn't just apply to food—you may want to teach this skill by leaving a dirty sock on the floor, which can also be very enticing to a dog.

Many of my clients ask, "How do I get my dog to leave things alone when I'm not around?" Understand that this is a *huge* step. You'll need to first spend many weeks training your dog not to steal. Doing that will create a foundation so that he'll at least have a clue what to do when he encounters, say, a meatloaf cooling on the counter and you're not there to tell him to stay away.

This reminds me of when I was a five-year-old kid. If my mother was cooking with her back turned, I would occasionally try to sneak a few cookies out of the cookie jar. Because she had three sons before me, my mom knew what was coming and was there to intercept me before I succeeded. After a while, I realized that my mom likely knew if I stole anything from the cookie jar, as she sold me on the fact that she was "all knowing." After all, if she was one step ahead of me in so many other instances, I figured she was probably one step ahead of me even when she wasn't around. Eventually, your dog will start thinking this way, too.

Until then, of course, set your dog up for success by always making sure he can't access the trash, food on the counter, or other goodies when you're not around.

BEGGING

Why dogs do this: Some dogs will try to steal food the second they think you're not looking—and then there are those who will just make you feel *really* guilty about not sharing. You know what I mean—begging is when your dog looks at you with those big, pathetic eyes that say, "I'm so hungry. Please feed me or I am going to collapse right now." And guess what happens when you cave in and slip him a morsel from the table? You're locking in this habit even further! Dogs become beggars by your feeding them while you eat. Period.

How to handle the behavior: In order to teach your dog not to beg, you'll first need to teach "settle," which is an indefinite "down/stay" where your dog just relaxes and/or takes a nap. You are basically teaching your dog what he *should* do instead of begging. "Settle" is different from "down" because you are not going to require your dog to be in an attentive "What's next?" state of mind. You want him to chill out instead. It's really helpful not only with begging, but also if you want your dog to, say, relax when you have company over or to give you some space when you're busy working.

"Settle" is best introduced when your dog is already in a relaxed mood, ideally after exercise. First, ask him to lie down, and then spend some time with him. Pet him softly. Encourage him to be calm as you would with a young child you were trying to settle down for some rest time. As your dog begins to relax, say "Settle" in a soft, soothing voice. Another great time to teach "settle" is when you catch your dog naturally doing this. Remember, this is called "capturing" a behavior.

Once your dog knows what "settle" means, you can set up training sessions to stop begging. In short, your goal is to instruct your dog to settle while you eat. Feeding your dog before you eat your meal will give you a head start—the less hungry he is, the less likely he'll beg. Also, start with small increments; for instance, maybe teach "settle" during a short snack time (say, you're eating an apple) and gradually work up to a full meal.

Ask your dog to settle, ideally before begging occurs. You may need to escort him to a particular place where he's comfortable, like his favorite bed in the same room. If he continually breaks the settle or continues to beg, say "No" and simply put him outside the room for a minute or two. Bring him back out and try again. You can reward your dog when he remains in a settle and doesn't beg during the meal. However, the timing of this reward is key in this case. When it comes to teaching your dog not to beg, the only acceptable time to reward with food is *after* dinner.

One last note: What if your dog starts begging and you don't want to make a training session of it at that moment? If that's the case, put him in another room until you are done with your meal so that begging does not go unchecked.

DIGGING

Why dogs do this: Some dogs may dig because something under the ground has caught the attention of their nose; others may dig a small area because the weather outside is too hot and the dirt they uncover offers a cool spot to lie in. However, in the vast majority of cases, dogs dig up the yard because they are moderate- to high-energy dogs who are straight-up bored.

How to handle the behavior: Of course, if you think your dog is digging holes just to keep cool, then bring the poor guy inside. Other than that, I cannot recall a single instance when regular, sufficient exercise hasn't resolved this issue. Teach your dog fetch and plenty of tricks, and make sure he has some suitable toys to play with. If you are unable to exercise your dog, then you will have to supervise him while outside and interrupt or prevent digging very consistently.

ASK *Zak*

Eating Poop

"My dog just ate his own feces. Is there something wrong with him?"

Believe it or not, this is a common behavior, called "coprophagia," Greek for "eating feces." Many dogs eat their own poop or other animal's droppings simply because they seem to enjoy it. Some experts say that dogs who eat feces may have a medical condition, or they're doing it because of natural instinct (female dogs will often eat their young offspring's feces as a way to clean the nest, and they'll lick their puppies' backsides to encourage them to eliminate). In my experience, coprophagia seems to be most common among dogs eighteen months or younger.

No matter what the cause, you need to stop this behavior! Needless to say, it's really gross. Also, it can be dangerous—if your dog eats the feces of another animal, he can pick up intestinal parasites or other bacteria. Of course, if your dog eats poop he can also transfer such bacteria to you, especially if he loves to give lots of kisses.

First, talk to your vet to rule out potential medical causes of coprophagia. Other than that, remember that the only way your dog can really get by with this behavior is if you are leaving him unattended or not controlling his environment. However, if you do catch your dog in the act, you need to interrupt the behavior, get his attention on you, and reward him when he complies. This is just a variation on the "leave it" you used for food and chewable items you don't want chewed.

Most dogs outgrow coprophagia naturally, but to end it sooner rather than later, supervise carefully when your dog is outside, and immediately pick up his waste. "Offer your dog a treat immediately after he poops, so he'll look forward to the treat in your hand rather than the one he just left behind," suggests Dr. Herron. And if your dog is raiding your cat's litter box—which many dogs like to do because cat food, which is very high in protein, seems to make cat poop very appealing—it's important to restrict his access to it by either putting it behind a cat door (as long as your dog can't fit through it) or raising it high enough so that only your cat can reach it.

▶ Chasing Cars

"Every time I walk my dog and a car passes by, he lunges for it. It's so scary! Why does he do this, and how can I get him to stop?"

This is a really common issue, especially among high-energy dogs who simply find moving things stimulating and worthy of chasing. Of course, this is a *very* dangerous habit, so it's crucial that you address it immediately and make sure your dog is in a tightly controlled setting as you work through it. (Also, chances are if your dog loves to chase cars that means he loves to chase anything and everything. This same drill applies whether your dog prefers to race after cars, joggers, or other animals.)

First, make sure your dog has gotten plenty of exercise so he's not raring to go and more likely to chase. Then it's a matter of taking a step back on your training and working on the "leave it/watch me" drill (see page 124, chapter 6). Until your dog is solid at doing that in various distracting scenarios that you control, you're not ready to move on.

When you have perfected that drill, head to your front yard or someplace with very light traffic so you don't overwhelm your dog. Have him on leash and ask him to "sit" and "stay" as a car drives by. Reward him with a treat if he does so. However, if your dog becomes too excited, loses all interest in the treats, and ignores you, or if he lunges for the car, you need to create distance from the street by, say, escorting your dog farther up the driveway toward your front door. Keep moving farther away until your dog complies. When he does, reward him liberally, and have him repeat the drill at the same spot to make sure he's got it.

Very slowly, over many training sessions, move closer and closer to the street, always keeping your dog on a very tight leash. Remember, patience is key—this issue can take several weeks or longer to resolve.

Humping

"My dog loves to hump other dogs, people's legs . . . just about anything. How can I get him to stop this?"

There are lots of different apparent reasons for this behavior, which is certainly normal among dogs. It does seem to be sexual, especially in young dogs who haven't been neutered or spayed. (Yes, female dogs hump, too!)

However, I also often see mounting behavior as a natural part of playtime among dogs of all ages, whether or not they've been "fixed." Dogs might hump when they get excited when interacting with other dogs or people, and they also might do this if they get anxious about a particular situation (say, meeting another dog for the first time or becoming a bit overwhelmed by the sheer number of dogs in a park). Some might hump their beds for a bit before settling down to rest, which is also very normal. Another possible reason: The dog simply never learned that humping is inappropriate behavior and, over time, it became a bad habit.

So what to do if you want to stop the humping, at least in certain situations? First, talk to your vet about the behavior to make sure the mounting isn't due to a medical issue, such as a urinary tract infection or priapism (persistent erections that may be painful). Neutering and spaying may help reduce the behavior as well, though you shouldn't rely on this alone to solve this issue. Next, start trying to determine when your dog usually humps, so you can preempt the behavior. So say your dog loves to hump every visitor who walks through your door. Remember that exercise greatly helps reduce unwanted behaviors, so make sure your dog plays fetch or at least goes for a long walk *before* the visit. Then, once the guest arrives, ask your dog to come to you and sit before the humping occurs, and reward accordingly with a treat or a little playtime. Do this every time, and your dog might not become as anxious or excited because he'll learn the ritual to expect when a new person enters your home.

What if your dog loves to hump a certain pillow on the couch? When you see him jump up next to it, immediately call him to you and provide him with an alternative behavior by asking him to sit. Again, reward him. Do the same thing when your dog starts circling and sniffing another dog and seems like he might mount him. Also, be extra careful: while mounting isn't an aggressive behavior, it might be construed as such by other dogs. As Dr. Herron explains, "Mounting directed at an unfamiliar dog can possibly become problematic if the receiver finds the action threatening."

Intervening ahead of time is absolutely key with humping, since it's a very natural behavior that becomes more solidified the more often it happens. You need to nip this one in the bud as soon as possible. As long as you are consistent with intercepting the behavior and redirecting it to a more acceptable one, you should be just fine!

CHAPTER EIGHT

IN SICKNESS AND IN HEALTH: BASIC CARE FOR YOUR DOG

Just like small children, dogs completely depend on us for their general well-being, from grooming and dental care to exercise and diet. Also, always protecting and caring for your pet will help you bond with her more than anything! According to the American Veterinary Medical Association, there are certain things you should do to keep your dog healthy, including feeding her a balanced diet, helping her maintain a healthy weight, making sure she gets enough exercise, neutering or spaying her, doing what you can to keep her parasite free, and taking her for annual vet visits to keep up with vaccinations and to detect any problems when they are most treatable.[1]

Your most important partner in keeping your dog healthy is your veterinarian. And I hope you chose one wisely, using the guidelines I outlined on page 45, chapter 2. While this chapter will give you an

overview of general health care issues, please always work with your vet
to determine what's best for *your* dog.

FOOD, GLORIOUS FOOD

Store-bought, homemade, vegetarian, gluten-free, grain-free, raw—
dogs have almost as many food options as humans do, and it can get
really confusing determining what's healthy and what's not. Marketing
tactics can get in the way, and if you ask other people their opinions,
everyone is going to give you different advice. For the most part, it's
a matter of personal preference. However, here are some things to
consider:

What Kind?

When I choose a dog food, I read the ingredient list, keeping in mind
that ingredients are listed in order of quantity. I always avoid brands
with inexpensive foods such as corn as the main ingredients and any
with questionable ingredients. Instead, I want the first ingredient to be
a quality protein such as chicken or fish.

In general, your selection should include a statement of nutritional adequacy that means the food is complete and balanced for your
pet's particular life stage according to the Association of American
Feed Control Officials (AAFCO). It should also include a guaranteed
analysis, which lists the percentages of the nutrients, and it must meet
certain requirements—at least minimum percentages of crude protein
and crude fat and maximum percentages of crude fiber and moisture.
Don't get fooled by sneaky marketing ploys—for instance, just as with
human food, many terms such as "whole foods" or "natural" haven't
been regulated, so they actually don't mean much when you see them
emblazoned on a bag. Instead, work closely with your vet to find the
best food based on your dog's age, size, activity level, and any particular health needs. Some people who work at pet supply stores are

also particularly knowledgeable and may be able to help. Or check out www.dogfoodadvisor.com for complete reviews of many brands.

Your vet can also help determine whether your dog would do better on dry food, wet food, or a combination of both. Also, if you're considering making your dog's food yourself, talk to your vet about what's right for your pet. Of course, your dog is going to have a say in the matter, too, so you may have a little trial and error until you find one that she loves.

How Often?

Puppies should eat two to three meals a day until they're around six months old. After that, you can feed your dog once or twice a day, depending on your dog's age, size, and exercise and eating habits. Some people free feed their dogs by pouring the daily food allotment into the bowl in the morning and letting their pets graze throughout the day. However, I find keeping a schedule is the best, especially when you're housetraining, as you can more easily predict when your dog will have to go outside to do her business. Also, in households with multiple dogs, scheduling is usually the only way to make sure that each dog is actually eating her own food.

How Much?

In terms of how much to feed your dog, you can start with the general recommendations on the bag, but it will vary tremendously based on your dog's age, size, metabolism, and exercise habits. A dog competing in agility competitions is going to need more calories than a dog who is the same age, breed, and size but a total couch potato. Talk to your vet about the ideal amount for your dog, and then watch your pet to make sure she remains a healthy weight. A good rule of thumb: You want to be able to feel her ribs, but you don't want to see them. If you notice your dog is getting too chunky, you can help her lose weight by limiting her portions, cutting back on treats, and increasing her exercise (all under the guidance of an expert, of course!).

Considering Food Allergies

Dogs can be allergic to a variety of foods; the most common offenders are beef, dairy, chicken, lamb, fish, eggs, corn, wheat, and soy. Of course, these allergies vary from dog to dog. Often if a dog is allergic to one ingredient, she may be allergic to others. Also, she may eat a certain food for months, even years, and then suddenly develop an allergy to it. Symptoms of a food allergy include vomiting, diarrhea, itchy skin and rear end, ear inflammation, and hot spots (red, moist, hot, irritated lesions on your dog's skin).

If you suspect your dog may be allergic to something she's eating, talk to your vet about a plan of action. He may prescribe a special hypoallergenic food and/or put your pet on an elimination diet to try to determine the culprit.

Raw Diets

There are a lot of trends when it comes to dietary options for dogs. For instance, you may have heard about BARF diets, which stands for either Bones and Raw Food or Biologically Appropriate Raw Food. The idea is that dogs should eat what their ancestors ate in the wild: raw meat, bones, and organs. Proponents claim that this kind of diet has health benefits such as shinier coats, cleaner teeth, healthier skin, and more energy, though no studies have backed that up. However, many veterinary experts as well as the American Veterinary Medical Association, the U.S. Centers for Disease Control and Prevention, and countless other organizations warn of the risks that come with a raw food diet for pets, such as the potential for *E. coli* and other food-borne illnesses and the dangers of bones perforating a dog's organs.[2] Also, a study in the *Journal of the American Veterinary Medical Association* evaluated raw diets and found that they had nutritional excesses or deficiencies that could cause serious health problems in dogs.[3]

Of course, it's up to you what kind of food you want to feed your dog. So if you feel strongly about putting your pet on a raw food diet, I urge you to work very closely with your veterinarian to make sure your dog is getting a well-balanced diet that won't harm her. However, I think the risks of a BARF diet far outweigh the potential benefits, and I recommend avoiding it.

GROOMING BASICS

Grooming is a critical element of caring for your dog; it can vary greatly depending on your dog's coat, age, and the area in which you live. Here's an overview:

Nails

It's very important to keep your dog's nails short. Not only can they scratch you and your furniture, but they can also snag on the carpet or even make it difficult for your dog to walk. However, cutting them appropriately can be tricky—cut too deep and you can cause your dog a lot of pain and excessive bleeding. If you want to do it yourself, ask your groomer or veterinarian to show you how to do so correctly.

Once you learn the proper technique, teach your dog to have a good association with having her nails trimmed. For instance, show her the nail clipper and allow her to smell it, then touch the nail trimmer to her nail, and then put the trimmer around it. Go slowly! Reward your dog after each small step if she behaves calmly, gradually working up to being able to cut the nail. She will learn to tolerate getting her nails trimmed in no time!

Teeth

We all know how important it is to brush our own teeth. Well, why would dogs be any different? Ideally, you should brush your dog's teeth daily. Doing so not only helps keep her breath fresh but also helps prevent periodontal disease (gum disease), which is common among dogs and, when left unchecked, has been associated with serious problems such as heart, liver, or kidney disease. Pick up a dog toothbrush or a finger brush from a pet supply store. Don't use human toothpaste, as it contains high-foaming detergents that a dog could swallow or inhale—they don't know to spit it out! Instead, experiment with different flavors of dog toothpaste until you find one your dog likes.

Also, make sure your dog has plenty of dental treats and soft toys to chew on as well as quality food—some products marked as "dental diets" include plaque- and/or tartar-reduction ingredients. Talk to your vet about the best food and treats for your dog based on her dental and other health needs.

The American Veterinary Dental College recommends that you ask your vet about plaque and tartar preventative options that can avert periodontal disease. Also, contact her if you notice signs of dental disease such as loose or discolored teeth, bad breath, any bleeding or sensitivity in the mouth, drooling, dropping food, and a loss of appetite or weight. During your dog's wellness exams—or during any vet visit, for that matter—your vet should also examine your dog's mouth to make sure it looks healthy.

Eyes

It's important to regularly look into your dog's eyes as a way of communicating with her. When you do so, if you notice any gunk buildup in the corners, wipe it away with a moist cotton ball. Make sure your dog's hair doesn't fall into her eyes, which can certainly irritate them. Call your vet if you notice any signs of an eye infection such as redness, cloudiness, excessive discharge, crusting, squinting, or a visible third eyelid (yes, dogs have three!)

If your dog has rusty-looking tearstains at the corner of her eyes, which can be particularly noticeable on white dogs, first visit your vet to determine a possible cause such as allergies or issues with the tear ducts. Then, if the stains bother you, talk to your vet about various options—for instance, pet supply stores carry products that you can sprinkle on your dog's food to possibly clear up the stains.

Ears

To clean your dog's ears, which you should ideally do once a week, you'll need cotton balls and a cleaning solution (ask your vet which one he recommends for your dog). Dab the outside of the earflap and then, with a new cotton ball, slowly work your way into the ear, stopping whenever you feel any resistance. If you notice that the cotton balls get very dirty, that could be a sign of an ear infection, so take your dog in for a medical exam. Other signs of an infection include discharge, crusting, an odor in the ear, redness, and swelling. Also, if your dog is scratching her ear a lot or rubbing it on the floor or other surfaces, or if she seems off balance, schedule an appointment to make sure everything is okay. She may have ear mites, a parasitic infection that can cause inflammation and irritation in the ear.

Coat

Some dogs need to be brushed every day to prevent matting and excessive shedding, others every few weeks or even less frequently. It's important to use the correct kinds of combs and brushes; your vet or a professional groomer can help you choose. Long-haired dogs may require a slicker brush and a bristle brush, while those with a smooth, short coat may need a bristle brush and a rubber brush.

You'll find that while some dogs love being brushed, others hate every second of it. If your dog falls into the latter category, go slowly. For example, first let your dog sniff the brush, then gently touch her with it, and work your way up to stroking her with the brush once. Reward every step of the way. Also, while you're brushing, check for fleas, flea dirt (flea droppings that look like little black specks), ticks, any lesions, irritated areas, or other issues with your dog's skin that may require medical attention. Always be gentle!

▶ **BATH TIME**

Some experts recommend bathing dogs weekly; others suggest less often, such as monthly. This is truly a matter of preference and lifestyle—for instance, if your dog sleeps in bed with you, you'll probably want to make extra sure she's clean and debris free. You can bathe your dog in a regular bathtub or a small portable plastic tub; some people even take their dogs into the shower with them! The key is to not get any water or shampoo in your dog's ears, eyes, or nose; don't just dump water on her head. You might want to carefully put cotton balls in your dog's ears to play it extra safe. Also, always use mild shampoos specifically designed for dogs; talk to your vet or groomer about which one is best for your dog. Lastly, if you are giving your dog regular baths—say, weekly—make sure her skin doesn't become irritated or flaky, which can be a sign that it's drying out; if that happens, either cut back on baths or choose a moisturizing shampoo that will help keep your dog's skin soft.

HIRING A PROFESSIONAL GROOMER

If you'd rather leave your dog's grooming needs to a professional, ask for recommendations from your vet as well as from friends, relatives, and neighbors with dogs. Some pet supply stores offer grooming on location, and the National Dog Groomers Association of America can also help you find groomers in your area. Besides cost, here are some other things to consider when shopping around:

- Does the groomer come to your house, or do you have to drop your dog off at a facility? Some groomers will even pick up your dog and drop her off at the end of the day.

- If it's a drop-off place, take a tour of the facility. Is the facility clean and odor free, and do the staff workers seem friendly? Ask to see a grooming in action if possible.

- Does the groomer ask for your vaccination records and emergency contact information? The groomer should do that and also readily supply references if you ask for them.

- Ask whether your dog will spend a lot of time in a cage and, if so, whether it provides ample room for her to move around.

- How does the groomer dry the dogs? Handheld hairdryers, stand dryers, or drying with a towel are best. If they use a dog-drying cage, which when used correctly can dramatically decrease drying time, make sure the unit is monitored at all times and that the groomer is highly trained. Dogs have died from overheating, dehydration, and/or burns after being left in the cages for too long or at temperatures that are too high.[4]

- No one national agency regulates or licenses pet groomers; however, check with the Better Business Bureau to see if any complaints have been filed against the grooming facility. Check reviews on sites such as www.yelp.com, too.

Spaying and Neutering

It's no secret how important it is to make sure your dog can't reproduce (unless you are a highly qualified professional breeder). Spaying typically removes a female dog's ovaries, fallopian tubes, and uterus, while neutering removes a male dog's testicles. Doing so helps reduce pet overpopulation: millions of unwanted dogs enter shelters annually, and many of them are euthanized. However, this is still a topic rife with controversy, and many myths about these surgeries persist. To set the record straight on a few of them, dogs are *not* more prone to gaining weight after being spayed or neutered, and male dogs won't suffer an identity crisis because they've lost their "manhood." Dogs gain weight because of too much food and too little exercise, and there's certainly no reason to think that dogs identify with their sexuality in the way humans do.

Of course, as with any medical procedure, there are some surgical and anesthetic risks involved, though the incidence of complications is very low.[5] On the other hand, these surgeries provide many important benefits to your dog: Spayed female dogs have lower odds of developing breast, uterine, and ovarian cancers later in life; neutered male dogs have a lower risk of prostate and testicular cancer, among other health problems.[6] Also, behavioral issues related to hormones such as scent marking, roaming, and humping may be reduced (though remember that training is how marking is usually resolved).

When's the best time to spay or neuter your pet? In females, typically before the first heat cycle if possible or before six months of age; in males, shoot for earlier than eight months (though healthy dogs can have the surgery much younger). Talk to your vet about the right time for *your* pet.

Signs You Need to Visit the Vet

Besides your annual checkups with your vet, schedule a visit if you notice any of the following symptoms:

- Vomiting

- Abnormal stools or potty habits

- Change in eating habits, loss of appetite, or excessive water consumption

- Discharge from the eyes, nose, or other body opening

- Any behavior that's out of the ordinary, such as excessive lethargy or sudden aggressiveness

- Excessive salivation

- Bald patches or any out-of-the-ordinary hair loss; dandruff

- Foul breath or foul odor coming from any part of the dog's body

- Any lumps, sores, or open wounds

- Difficultly getting up and lying down or any limping

- Excessive licking, biting, or scratching any body part, or head shaking

Vaccinations

Like humans, dogs need certain vaccinations to keep them safe from illnesses that can otherwise cause very serious symptoms. One example: Parvovirus is a highly contagious viral illness that can cause vomiting; lethargy; severe, often bloody diarrhea; and dehydration. It can even lead to death.

However, vaccines do come with some health risks, such as soreness and allergic reactions, so you should work with your veterinarian to determine exactly what *your* dog needs. A puppy should start receiving core vaccinations around six weeks and then every three weeks until she's sixteen weeks old (with the exception of rabies, which is administered once between twelve and sixteen weeks at a minimum). Adult dogs need to be revaccinated every one to three years; your vet will determine how often based on the vaccine, your dog's particular health, and her environment.

In 2011, the American Animal Hospital Association updated its guideline recommendations for dog vaccines. They list the "Core" vaccines—the ones universally recommended—and "Noncore" vaccines, which are optional based on your dog's exposure. Again, work with your vet to determine which ones your dog needs. Here's a breakdown:

CORE
Canine distemper virus
Canine adenovirus 2
Canine parvovirus 2
Rabies

Bordetella

Leptospirosis

Lyme disease

Canine parainfluenza virus

Canine influenza

Measles (puppies younger than six weeks or breeding females)

PARASITES

From fleas and ticks to worms and *Giardia*, all dogs are susceptible to various different parasites throughout their lifetime. Here's an overview.

External Parasites: Fleas and Ticks

The notorious enemy of all dogs, fleas have long caused serious problems for both animals and humans alike. (They are responsible for plague!) Fleas are wingless insects that jump from host to host and feed on them. They can cause problems for dogs such as anemia, tapeworm (when a flea carrying tapeworm eggs is ingested), and allergic reactions.

If your dog gets fleas—some signs including excessive scratching or biting of the skin, hair loss, hot spots, and flea dirt, which looks like specks of dirt but is actually flea droppings—first call your vet to determine an immediate treatment plan for your dog. Treatment might include a special shampoo or topical liquid that will kill the fleas and their eggs. Then contact a local exterminator to discuss options for banishing the pests from your yard; these experts can also tell you other ways to eliminate the fleas from your home, based on how bad the infestation is. For instance, first steps could be washing all bedding in hot water and vacuuming every carpet and then disposing of the vacuum bag.

Ticks, on the other hand, are arachnids. Like fleas, they will suck the blood out of their host, which can lead to anemia; they also transmit very dangerous illnesses such as Lyme disease, Rocky Mountain spotted fever, and *Ehrlichia*. If you notice a tick on your dog, put on a pair of disposable gloves, wipe the area with rubbing alcohol, and carefully remove the tick with a pair of tweezers. Make sure you pull the tick straight out (don't twist it!) and check that you don't leave any part of the critter behind. You should preserve the tick in a closed container with rubbing alcohol so if your dog does fall ill in the coming weeks, your vet can know which type of tick was the culprit. Wash the site where the tick was on your dog thoroughly and call your vet to discuss a further course of action.

For both fleas and ticks, yearly prevention is your best bet—there are topical medications and oral pills, many of which are a two-for-one combo that prevent both parasites. Also, keep your dog's bedding and living area clean and check her regularly for fleas and ticks, especially if you live in a humid or woody area.

Internal Parasites: Worms, Giardia, and Coccidia

Unfortunately, in addition to being susceptible to external parasites, all dogs are also susceptible to internal parasites that can lead to a whole slew of health problems. The key is to work closely with your doctor to prevent these parasites if possible or treat them as soon as you notice any symptoms.

Here's a breakdown:

HEARTWORM

These are parasitic roundworms that live in the arteries and heart of an animal; they can grow as long as twelve inches and live up to seven years. The worm spreads from animal to animal via mosquito bites and can include symptoms such as weight loss, coughing, and difficulty breathing; it can eventually lead to heart failure, lung disease, even death. While heartworms are most prevalent in areas prone to mosquitos—such as along the Gulf of Mexico, the Atlantic Ocean coastline, and along the Mississippi River—it has been reported in all fifty states.[7]

According to the Food and Drug Administration (FDA), there are two drugs approved to treat heartworm disease; however, both are very costly and can be toxic for dogs. Instead, year-round prevention is the best medicine. The FDA has approved several products for safe, effective prevention of heartworm disease: such products are available as a topical liquid, oral tablets, or an injectable. Talk to your vet about which type is best for your dog.

OTHER WORMS

Roundworms, tapeworms, hookworms, and whipworms all live in the intestines of dogs, and they can cause serious issues ranging from weight loss and diarrhea to life-threatening anemia and lethargy. Roundworms and hookworms are also zoonotic, which means that they can be transmitted from an animal to a human. Notify your vet if your dog has diarrhea, a change in her appetite or coat, or excessive coughing. You may also notice the worms in your dog's stool or under her tail.

While the deworming that your dog probably got as a puppy will get her off to a good start, it's still important to take further steps to protect your dog. For instance, tapeworms are passed to dogs from infected fleas, so a flea prevention regimen is key. The medicine you give your dog for heartworm prevention will likely also protect against most worms. What about protecting you and the other people in your family? Good hygiene, such as washing your hands as needed, will help ensure that if your dog ever does have worms, she won't pass them on to you.

GIARDIA AND COCCIDIA

When swallowed, these highly contagious, zoonotic, single-celled parasites can damage your dog's intestinal lining and limit the amount of nutrients she gets from food; they can also cause diarrhea. Fortunately, when detected, they can be eliminated with medication.

ASK *Zak*

Helping the Medicine Go Down

*"My dog absolutely hates taking medicine. Any tips on how to get
her to take a pill?"*

Just like humans, some dogs take pills and other forms of medicine
without a fight. Others seem to have a lot of difficulty with it. While
there's not a surefire "spoonful of sugar" technique that will work
across the board, there are some tricks that can help. First, ask your
vet if she has a chewable version of the medication. If not, hide the pill
in a bit of wet dog food or inside a piece of soft meat, peanut butter, or
cheese. You can also try using a special treat designed specifically to
hide pills. However, plenty of clever dogs will catch on pretty quickly—
they may somehow eat all their food and purposely avoid the pill, or
they'll chew up the treat and spit the pill back out. If that's the case,
gently open your dog's mouth, put the pill at the base of her tongue,
close her mouth and tilt it back until she swallows. If you think your
dog might bite you, ask your vet for alternatives.

Poisoning

*"My dogs just got into my trash and ate the remainder of the
chocolate cake we threw out. I've heard chocolate is toxic for dogs.
What should I do?"*

Call your nearest poison control center or the ASPCA Animal Poison
Control (888-426-4435), and get to your vet right away. I know some
people might want to take a wait-and-see approach, but even a small
amount of chocolate can be toxic to a dog, and it's difficult for medical
experts to determine how your dog is doing over the phone. The same

goes for other toxins, ranging from raisins and houseplants to prescription meds and common household cleaners. (See page 37, chapter 2, for a reminder on which foods and other items are dangerous to dogs.) Getting your dog help immediately can also mean a better prognosis for her.

Do not try to self-treat your dog or induce vomiting unless your vet or poison expert specifically tells you do to so. However, when you do get to the vet, it can be helpful if you can bring a sample and/or packaging of whatever item your dog ingested.

Hot Weather

"I live in a state where it's hot and humid all summer long. How do I help my dog handle the heat?"

I totally understand this question—I live in New Orleans, where the summer weather can be downright sweltering and stifling. Just as you take measures to protect yourself from the elements, it's important to do the same for your dog. Here's what to do:

- Make sure your dog has an unlimited supply of water and, if she has to spend any time outside, plenty of shade.

- Your dog's exercise needs don't suddenly dwindle during hot spells. However, you'll probably need to make modifications. For instance, play fetch or go for long walks first thing in the morning or at dusk when temperatures may be a little cooler. Also, if your dog is, say, used to going for a five-mile run with you in the morning, you might want to scale back on that a bit until you're sure she's accustomed to the weather. Of course, always bring lots of extra water with you.

- I *always* advise against leaving your dog in a car unattended. However, that recommendation is especially crucial during summer months when the temperature in the car can rapidly skyrocket and feel like an oven. Don't underestimate how quickly that can happen: According to the American Veterinary

Medical Association, the temperature in your car can rise twenty degrees in only ten minutes, thirty degrees in twenty minutes, and so on. Even if it's a comfortable eighty degrees outside, after thirty minutes it can be 114 degrees in the car.[8] In such temperatures, dogs can become severely dehydrated; some suffer brain damage and many die. Cracking the window, even a few inches, doesn't help. Just don't leave your dog in the car alone. If you have to go somewhere and you can't bring your dog inside with you, then leave her at home.

- Whenever possible, walk your dog in the shade or on the grass. Asphalt, metal, and other substances can burn the pads on her paws.

- Make sure your dog has a fresh haircut, but don't shave her—a dog's fur can help protect her from the heat and from sunburns.

- Don't forget about sunscreen! If your dog has any bald patches or little hair, make sure you lather her with protective lotion before you head out. Dogs' noses and ears are also susceptible to sunburn. Talk to your vet about the best kind of sunscreen for your dog.

Cold Weather

"I live in an area where winters are bitterly cold. Any tips on protecting my dog that time of year?"

Just as with excessively hot weather, cold weather climates come with their own set of potential dangers for dogs. Of course, how much your dog can tolerate will depend on her coat, size, age, amount of body fat, and overall health. Here are some safety precautions you can take:

- Know the dangers of antifreeze: it's a sweet substance that dogs may find tasty, but even a tiny amount can poison your pet. Clean up any spills immediately.

- If you live in an area where it snows, there will likely be salt on the sidewalks. Wipe your dog's paws whenever you come into the house—the salt can irritate the pads of her feet and make her sick if she licks it. She may also have antifreeze or other chemicals on her paws that you need to remove.

- Don't let your dog eat the snow—again, it can contain chemicals that could be toxic to her.

- Always keep your pet on a leash, especially during a snowstorm, and make sure she's wearing her ID tags at all times. More dogs are lost in winter than in any other season.[9]

- If your dog has short hair and will tolerate clothing, consider getting her a coat or sweater that will keep her extra warm. Booties can help keep her paws toasty, too.

- Make sure your dog still gets plenty of exercise in cold weather (always keeping her safety in mind, of course). In fact, many dogs love the snow, so bundle up and get outside. What if you or your dog just can't handle the cold? The good news is that there are plenty of indoor classes for dogs. See page 208, chapter 9, to learn more about such options.

Losing Teeth

"I'm always finding my puppy's little teeth around the house—I even found her chewing on one the other day. Is this normal?"

Yes, it's normal. Dogs start developing twenty-eight baby teeth (also known as deciduous) at around three weeks of life. However, by four months these super-sharp tiny teeth start falling out to make room for forty-two permanent adult teeth. Whereas a child will take years to lose all her baby teeth, a dog will go through the process in a matter of months. You might find the teeth throughout the house, but chances are you never will. Many dogs swallow them, and that's okay. Of course, call your vet if your dog loses a permanent tooth for any reason or if you notice that she has any retained teeth—that is, a baby tooth that stays in place even after the permanent tooth has erupted.

These retained teeth can force the permanent teeth to grow at abnormal angles and can also lead to tooth decay, so your vet may have to extract them.

Fear of the Vet

"My dog starts shaking and whimpering anytime I get near the vet's office. What should I do to make her more comfortable on visits?"

Think about it from your dog's perspective. Imagine if every time you went to a particular place you got poked and probed and possibly had to endure multiple injections. Now imagine that you didn't understand that the people doing this to you were only trying to keep you healthy. Well, that's how it is for dogs (just as it is for very young children), and it's no wonder many of them seem to downright despise vet visits. Some get really anxious beforehand and may tremble or cry. Others have to be literally carried into the office, because otherwise they wouldn't set one paw through the door.

I'm not going to promise you that you can help any dog love her visits to the vet. However, you can take steps to make them a little easier for her:

- First, make sure you choose a vet who has a good bedside manner. An extra gentle touch or soothing voice can help calm your dog.

- See page 66, chapter 3, for suggestions on making your dog comfortable during vet visits from day one (which may also help dogs who have already developed a fear of the vet).

- Take your dog on trips to your vet's office at times when she doesn't have an appointment. Ask your vet and the other staff members to shower your dog with lots of affection and treats. By doing this, your dog won't always have a negative association with going to the vet. It's as though she starts to realize, "Hey, this place can be kind of fun!"

- If your dog seems truly anxious or fearful about her vet visits—some signs include trembling, growling, snapping, or panting—talk to your vet about what else you can do to help settle her nerves.

In Case of an Emergency

No one likes to think about it, but it's always important to be prepared in case your dog becomes seriously ill or injured. Doing so can help you stay calm in case of an emergency; this, in turn, can lead to a much better prognosis for your pet.

Here's a Checklist of Things to Do:

- Keep important numbers taped to your refrigerator, saved in your phone, or somewhere else that's easily accessible. Include your vet's number and address and the number and address for your emergency clinic. Also include the ASPCA Animal Poison Control twenty-four-hour hotline number (888-426-4435). There may be a slight charge for the call, but it can save your dog's life.

- Call your veterinarian immediately. If the office is closed, contact your emergency vet clinic. If you're not sure whether or not your dog needs to be seen, always err on the side of caution.

- Keep a first aid kit on hand for your dog. You may want to include hydrocortisone cream, tape and gauze, saline wash, antiseptic wipes, and a rectal thermometer and petroleum. Of course, you should call your vet if your dog has sustained a serious injury, but with these supplies you can at least help manage symptoms until you can get her to the office.

- If you have to transport your dog, do so very carefully. Ideally, have someone else drive so you can tend to your pet. Keep your dog warm and safe, ideally in a travel crate if possible. Also, be extra careful—even the friendliest dog may snap or nip if she's in pain and scared.

DISASTER PREPAREDNESS

It's always important to have a disaster preparedness plan in place for your loved ones in the event of a fire, tornado, hurricane, or other natural disaster. However, it's crucial that you include your pet in that plan. During Hurricane Katrina, I saw firsthand what can happen to animals during these catastrophes. Far too many dogs and other pets were stranded and never reunited with their people; many others starved to death or drowned. Having a preestablished protocol for such situations can help ensure that every member of your family, including the furry ones, stays safe and sound.

Here are some things you can do:

- If you have to evacuate your home, try your best to never leave your pet behind. If at all possible, take her with you or arrange other accommodations. Many disaster shelters will not accept pets, so keep that in mind; know of pet-friendly motels or hotels that you might stay in, a boarding facility or a veterinarian who will take your dog, or relatives or friends who will pet sit in a pinch.

- Make sure your dog is microchipped and always wearing her identification tags.

- Put together a pet emergency preparedness kit—assemble your dog's food, bottled water, bowls, any medication your dog takes, and a leash in a sturdy bag or container. Include a good recent photo of your dog, in case she gets lost during an emergency. Keep this kit, along with your dog's first aid kit, somewhere safe and easily accessible so you can bring it with you if you have to leave your home in a hurry (or head to a safe room in your house during, say, a tornado).

- Run through a fire drill with your family and include your pet as part of it.

- Consider purchasing a pet rescue window decal—a bright sticker you put on your home's front window, which alerts emergency workers, policemen, or firefighters that you have a pet inside. The decals are available at pet supply stores and many online retailers.

- Learn more about disaster plans that include your pet at www.ready.gov and www.redcross.org. Being prepared can save your dog's life.

CHAPTER NINE

TIME FOR FUN: COOL TRICKS, TRAVELING, EXERCISE, AND MORE

Raising a dog is certainly a lot of hard work and responsibility, but it can be a total blast, too. In fact, it should be! Teaching your dog tricks, getting him involved in dog sports, and finding other fun things to do together can be beneficial for him in so many ways. First, spending more time with your dog and teaching him new concepts simply helps you learn to communicate better with one another. Also, since these activities are entertaining and even amusing at times, many people particularly enjoy teaching them. That relaxed good mood, in turn, helps strengthen your bond—a critical ingredient if you hope to have an exceptionally behaved dog.

Another advantage is that tricks and other activities teach your dog to think outside the box. It's like advanced math for high school students. Even if a person doesn't require the knowledge of, say, calculus or trigonometry long term, learning it strengthens the brain and helps one become a better thinker. This is what tricks and extracurricular activities are to your dog (though probably more enjoyable than some of those math classes, in my opinion!). You should engage in additional creative training simply to keep your dog mentally content. This is especially true if you have a moderate- to high-energy dog—these dogs are usually very smart and they love to learn, so if you don't give their energy and curiosity an outlet, they may wind up with behavioral issues. For those of you with these types of dogs, this chapter may not be optional.

Tricks and dog sports are just part of the story. Remember, your dog is now a family member, one you should incorporate into your life as much as possible. That could mean taking him on road trips or other family vacations, or simply spending the afternoon in the pool on a hot day. You might want your pet to join you on your morning run, or you could be interested in taking him hiking. In this chapter, I'll walk you through all of these options and more, so that you and your dog can have an exciting and rewarding life together.

SUPER-FUN TRICKS

Basic training skills such as "sit" and "come" are nonnegotiables that our dogs should know. These basics are the equivalent to teaching a young child to stay quiet while you're on a business call and to not run into the street without looking both ways. Tricks, on the other hand, are like teaching your child to play the piano or hit a baseball. They may be optional, but they'll definitely enrich his life.

When you're ready to teach your dog a new trick, first get him mentally warmed up. For example, I'll start off a training session with a basic "sit" and a few other skills I know the dog has perfected, and I'll reward generously for the heck of it. This gets him psyched up about training. I also keep the mood light and optimistic. I even say, "I am going to teach you something new, okay?" in a very sincere way. Over time, your dog will learn exactly what this means.

As for rewards, feel free to give your dog one every time he does a trick. Whereas you'll likely want to wean off the rewards for the basic skills, it's fine to always give a treat or a little playtime when your pet does something extra special. Lastly, remember that not every trick is meant for every dog, so try a bunch and see what sticks. Sometimes your dog will pick up on a new trick very quickly, but other times it may take quite a few training sessions. Be patient! Here's how to teach some of my favorite tricks.

▶ Shake

This is the easiest trick ever, especially since many dogs will offer their paw naturally. If your dog does, all you might have to do is reward him when he does so and say "Shake" (or an alternative such as "Paw") so he begins correlating the word to the trick. This is called "capturing" a behavior. Eventually, your dog will understand that the word and the trick are connected, and you can ask for the trick *before* he performs it instead of saying the word after the fact.

If your dog doesn't do shake naturally, you can still teach it to him. Here's what to do:

1. Ask your dog to sit. Then tickle the back of his front legs a bit. Most dogs will move their paw ever so slightly here; that's when you enthusiastically say "Yes!" and follow up with a reward. It's important to reward for the smallest move in the right direction at first, even if your dog does it accidentally.

2. Continue this exercise and encourage your dog with a "Yes!" and a treat every time he shows he's on the right track. Soon he'll likely conclude that movements of his paw are what's working. Once he sees that even a slight movement results in an awesome outcome, he'll be a bit more eager to try to do what you're asking him to do. You'll notice a gradual progression from slight movements to more pronounced, deliberate ones, usually in one to two sessions. When you are happy that the movement your dog is making is pretty close to the final trick, say "Shake" just prior to your dog's offering his paw, so he starts correlating the word with what he's doing.

3. Some dogs will alternate which paw they offer, especially at first. Reward for both, at least initially.

▶ Play Dead

This is the trick where your dog lies down on his side or back when you ask and looks like he's pretending to be dead. It's a classic crowd pleaser! It's impressive because it seems complicated, but it really isn't. You get a lot of bang for your buck on this one. Here's what to do:

1. "Play dead" is easiest taught using lure training, which I explained on page 125, chapter 6. Start off by letting your dog know you have an amazing treat that he really loves. Ask him to lie down. If your dog still hasn't perfected "down," you may have to lure him into position. Remember to hold the treat really close to his nose—I find it helpful to pretend that the treat and your dog's nose are magnets. If the two are too far apart, the "magnetic connection" is lost.

2. Once your dog is lying down on his stomach, move the treat to the left or right and then over his shoulder, but still very close to his nose. Experiment with both sides, as some dogs are more likely to go in one direction than another. Go slowly! (Almost everyone goes too fast here at first.) Keep moving the treat until your dog is lying down on his side and settled in that position for a couple of seconds. It will take a few tries before your dog understands what you want him to do. As your dog performs a rough draft of the trick, say something like "Yes! Play dead," so that you now have a phrase to pair with the behavior.

3. After you've done this a few times and your dog seems to be getting the picture, next lure with the treat a bit farther away from your dog's face. If you're seeing success, this is also a good time to begin to use a primitive hand signal with your luring hand. Think of this as half hand signal and half lure. Any subtle variation from a lure into something resembling your own version

of what the hand signal will become is what you are looking for here. Over time, you can gradually evolve this hand signal into anything you want. The thing about hand signals is that they should be individual to you and your dog.

4. Over the next two to ten training sessions, polish up the trick as you wish. A common variant is making a pretend gun with your hand as the hand signal and saying "Bang!" instead of "Play dead." This will get you extra laughs, and your dog will relish the attention.

Roll Over

"Roll over" is simply "play dead" 2.0 in many respects. Here's what to do:

1. Follow the steps I just outlined for "play dead." However, instead of pausing at the "play dead" position, continue luring your dog until he rolls over all the way. Reward for even a millimeter of extra movement here at first. It is totally normal for some dogs to resist rolling over, especially if they've already learned "play dead," since they may be thinking, "I know this one!"

2. Be patient as your dog works through the confusion, and encourage him to make it the whole way over by using a treat and lots of enthusiasm. This may take some time. Whatever you do, do not physically force your dog to roll over. It is super-common for people to do this, but this sets back "roll over" training because most dogs hate being forced onto their backs. If your dog is particularly resistant, you'll just need to put in some extra training.

3. As soon as your dog makes it the whole way over, say "Yes, roll over!" and give him the treat. Celebrate for a moment and then immediately try again in an attempt to build momentum on your progress. Over time, focus on introducing a custom hand signal (such as making a small circle with your finger) as you progressively move the treat farther away.

▶ Speak

Getting your dog to bark when you ask him to speak is super-cute. "Speak" comes a lot more naturally for some dogs than for others. If your dog is a big barker, then this one may be easy for him. If he's more reluctant, be extra patient. Here's what to do:

1. First, it's especially important to use a strong currency that your dog really loves. For this trick, my default currency is real meat. However, if you have a toy-obsessed dog, then a toy he absolutely goes crazy for can work, too, provided you've taught him to "sit" and "stay" for this toy.

2. Stand in front of your dog presenting the potential reward. Simply wait at first. If your dog is super-interested in the reward, don't give it to him at first.

3. Now be patient. The idea is to wait until your dog barks as if he's saying, "What are you waiting for? Give me the treat already!" at which time you should say "Yes, speak!" and reward promptly. This can take anywhere from a few seconds or minutes to several training sessions.

4. Incorporate a hand signal of your choice when you tell your dog "Speak."

▶ Back Stall

This is my go-to trick when I need to teach a dog something impressive, flashy, and awe-inspiring. In fact, when filming the pilot episode of my TV show *SuperFetch*, this was the trick I selected to teach my first guest on the show. Also, when Venus and I made an appearance on *Late Night with Jimmy Fallon*, this was one of the tricks I had her do with Jimmy!

What's a back stall? It's where your dog literally jumps on your back and stays there. Obviously, there are limitations to this trick—if you have any back issues or if your dog is particularly heavy, you should probably skip it. Also, you'll want to have sufficient padding on your back, such as a thick sweatshirt, since dogs have nails that can be sharp. Take care to practice this in a grassy or padded area, and know that while very small dogs can do this too, you may just need to stay extra close to the ground. Here's what to do:

1. To get started, use a table, chair, bench, or other solid platform for your dog to stand on. The height should be low enough for your dog to easily jump on, and it's critical that the platform be very stable as dogs often tend to become nervous about standing on shaky things. Teach your dog to jump onto the platform by encouraging him to do so with a treat or toy and plenty of good energy. It's common for many dogs to jump on and then immediately off, perhaps touching the platform with only two paws. At first, reward any small success to show your dog he's on the right track. Gradually encourage him to stay on the platform until you tell him to get down.

2. Once your dog jumps onto the platform with all four paws, say "Yes!" and reward vigorously. Next, ask him to stay for one or two seconds. Say "Stall" so he starts to associate the word with the action.

3. Next, it's time to encourage your dog to climb or jump on top of your back. I advise having a friend help you do this if possible, though it's not necessary. First, support yourself on all fours so that your back resembles a tabletop. Keep your back level and encourage your dog to jump onto it. This process can be really awkward, so again, reward for every tiny success. Even if your dog gets only one paw on your back, reward him in the beginning stages. Remember, you're taking a step back when you change a variable, which, in this case, is jumping on your back instead of the platform. Your dog may be a bit confused at first. This is normal.

4. The first magic moment to look for is when all four paws touch your back simultaneously, even if just for a brief moment. Celebrate this as though your dog has mastered the trick! Get a feel for how comfortable he is with all four paws on your back over the next many attempts. As he progresses, your goal is to increase the amount of time he spends with all four paws on

your back before you ask him to get down. What a fun way to practice "stay!"

5. ▶ The goal, at first, is to have your dog stand on your straight, stable back. Truthfully, that trick alone will knock the socks off of people, and you may see no reason to take it a step further. However, for those of you feeling ambitious, you can add an extra "wow" factor: Once your dog seems very comfortable standing on your flat back, you can try standing up slowly so that your back is at a forty-five-degree angle. Or if you've taught your dog to "sit pretty", this can be a great way to combine two awesome tricks. This trick was how Venus and I used to open the show when we performed with Stunt Dog Productions years ago, and it always got the crowd fired up. If you get good at this, you should easily be able to schedule an appearance on your local morning news to show off, too!

TRAVELING WITH YOUR DOG

Why leave your dog at home when you can take him with you? From car rides to air travel, here's how to keep your pet safe and happy when you're on the go.

Car Rides

I've driven all over the United States with my dogs, and they have really come to accept the car as an extension of our house. In fact, all of my dogs always hop into the car and relax immediately. However, it's important to take steps to make sure your dog is comfortable during car rides:

- As always, safety first. Never let your dog sit in the passenger seat—if the airbag goes off, it can kill him. Instead, use a crate in the back of the car, which is the safest way to transport your pet. Just make sure you've introduced the crate properly and that your dog is comfortable with it *before* you head out on a long car trip. Another option: a special doggy booster seat or harness that attaches to the seat belt in the back of the car. You can find these at pet supply stores and through online retailers.

- Just like humans, dogs can get carsick—especially puppies or young dogs, because their inner ears haven't fully developed yet. Also, adult dogs who haven't traveled much in a car might get nauseous because of motion sickness or anxiety about the ride. Take precautions such as not feeding your dog a big meal right before getting in the car and making sure you bring towels or an old blanket so that if he does get sick, cleanup will be a lot easier.

- Your dog is more likely to relax during a three-hour car ride if he's already been acclimated to the car for ten to twenty minutes at a time. Gradually increase the time so that he'll more easily adjust to a longer car ride. Also, if you take him in the car only when he's going to the vet or the groomer, he may have a negative association with it. The more experiences your dog has with going to a happy place, like the park or a pet supply store, the more eagerly he'll get in the car.

- During your road trip, plan on stopping at least every three to four hours (more often if your dog is young or very small). Let your dog play some fetch or take an extended walk. You need to stretch your legs and use the bathroom—and so does your dog.

- Never leave your dog unattended in a car. Because temperatures in a closed car can quickly soar in warm months and can plummet in cold ones, many dogs have died when left even for just a few minutes. Also, personally I wouldn't risk it—lots of dogs are snatched when left unattended.

- As tempting as it is, don't let your dog stick his entire head out the window while you're driving. He can get hit with foreign objects, flying debris, and dust particles. Also, his ears can suffer damage from flopping in the wind, his eyes can suffer abrasions, or he could fall out of the car altogether. Instead, crack the window open a bit so he can enjoy all the fascinating and different smells during the journey. Hey, for them that's half the fun!

Air Travel

Small dogs are allowed to fly in the cabin on many commercial airlines if they can fit in a travel case and under the seat in front of you. However, if you're planning a trip, make sure you call ahead of time—most flights can accommodate only a limited number of pets, and some airlines won't allow animals when going to certain destinations. You may have to pay an extra fee, which can be around $100 or more (twice that, if you're flying round-trip). Confirm the dimensions of the pet carrier the airplane can accommodate, and know that your pet and the carrier often count as your carry-on. Also, check what kind of paperwork you have to bring. For instance, some airlines require proof of recent vaccinations or a health certificate. Lastly, keep in mind that some dogs are less suitable for flying than others, especially ones who are older or brachycephalic (dogs with pushed-in faces such as Pugs). Talk to your vet about whether or not your dog can handle flying. Other things you can do to help the trip go smoothly:

- Exercise your dog before the flight to make sure he's tired so that he may sleep during the flight or at least not have so much nervous energy. Also, make sure he relieves himself before you get on board.

- You should carry or walk your pet through security while the carrier goes through the X-ray machine. However, at any other time you will have to keep your dog in the carrier.

- Once on board, give your dog a favorite toy that will keep him occupied during the flight. Talk to him in a calm voice and let him know he's safe. If he starts to cry, he may be anxious, so sneak him a treat or two to communicate that you're there for him and that this isn't so bad. Just never open the carrier enough that he can get out!

- Bring a leash and a bowl so you can give your dog some water and take him for a well-deserved walk the second you're able.

While a small dog can usually travel on board with you, larger dogs cannot. So if you have, say, a forty-pound dog and want to fly with him, you'll have to either check him as baggage on your flight (on which he'll fly in the cargo hold) or have him fly as cargo on a separate flight, depending on the airline. Are these options safe? To be honest, they may not be. Major organizations such as the Humane Society of the United States strongly recommend that people avoid taking their dogs on planes, particularly if that means the dog has to travel in the cargo hold.[1] Also, according to the United States Department of Transportation, each year many animals who travel in cargo die; others are injured or lost.[2]

However, I understand that sometimes you have no choice. I once flew with Venus to appear on *Late Night with David Letterman* years ago. She is about thirty-five pounds, so I couldn't bring her on board, driving would have taken too much time since it was last minute, and I obviously couldn't leave her home! This was very early on in my career, and to be honest it really stressed me out. Fortunately, Venus was fine; however, ever since then I have insisted on driving my dogs everywhere. Once I even drove with Venus from Atlanta to Los Angeles to do a five-minute appearance for the Television Critics Association. A few weeks later, I drove round-trip from Atlanta to New York twice in two weeks to appear on *The Rachael Ray Show* and *Late Night with Jimmy Fallon* in order to avoid flying.

If you have to fly with your dog and check him as baggage or have him fly alone as cargo, definitely contact the airlines to learn of any restrictions. For instance, the federal Animal Welfare Act enforced by the U.S. Department of Agriculture (USDA) won't allow pets to fly unless they are at least eight weeks old and weaned. The animals also must be protected from direct sunlight, and they must not be exposed to temperatures above 85°F and below 45°F for more than forty-five minutes when being moved to and from the airplane to the terminal (though, in the case of the latter, a vet could sign a certificate stating that the dog is acclimated to cold climates).[3] Also, talk to your vet to make sure your dog's fit for traveling—some airlines don't allow brachycephalic breeds to fly in the cargo hold at all. Most airlines have a special department or call center that will thoroughly brief you on what to expect, so contact them as well. Here's what else you can do to help make your dog's experience as pleasant as possible:

- Find a secure, well-constructed pet transport kennel to transport your dog. According to the USDA, no particular kennels have been preapproved by the airlines, the airline associations, or the USDA themselves, so any such claims are false advertising.[4] Instead, find a well-constructed, secure kennel and get your dog accustomed to it well before he's scheduled to fly.

- Book direct nonstop flights only. Avoid very busy travel days and peak hours. The less chaos and fewer changes, the safer and less hectic it will be for your dog.

- Make sure your dog is microchipped and that all of his identification tags are secure. The kennel he's traveling in should also have all of your contact information.

- The International Air Transport Association recommends avoiding the use of tranquilizers or other forms of sedation to calm a dog during a flight. If you really think your dog needs this, talk to your vet.

Pet-Friendly Accommodations

When you travel with your pet, you may need to find overnight accommodations that will accept him. Luckily, it's not that difficult—so many hotels and motels are pet-friendly nowadays. Many popular hotel chains accommodate pets. Also, websites such as www.bringfido.com can help you find dog-friendly hotels in your area. However, if you're considering a particular hotel, call ahead of time to find out about any restrictions. Some hotels allow only dogs up to a certain size or require that you stay on the lowest floor. Many charge a pet fee. Ask about perks, too—some hotels offer treats, special bedding, bowls, and even pet-sitting or pet-walking services for their furry guests.

Another option: Consider renting. Through sites such as www.vrbo.com, www.homeaway.com, and www.airbnb.com, you can rent anything from a tiny studio apartment to a multimillion-dollar estate. Some places require that you stay for a week or longer, but many allow you to rent for just a night or two. Rates run the gamut, but you can likely find a place that fits your budget. A little secret: A lot of rentals say they won't allow pets, but if you fall in love with a particular place it's worth a call; many owners will make exceptions, especially if you have a small, well-behaved dog.

EXERCISE

As I explained in chapter 4, age-appropriate exercise is one of the principles of my training program. It's important for dogs in so many ways— it reduces unwanted behaviors such as digging and chewing, helps them sleep better at night, keeps their weight in check, and increases mobility as they get older. However, each dog can handle a different amount of exercise, so talk to your vet about what's ideal for yours. If your dog has a lot of energy, you'll almost certainly want to schedule at least twenty minutes to an hour of exercise daily.

So what kind of exercise? The critical thing is that the form of exercise you choose should involve *you*. In fact, it turns out that exercising together is an indicator that *you'll* get the physical activity you need. A study in the *American Journal of Public Health* found that people who have dogs have as much as 77 percent higher odds of getting enough physical activity as compared with those who don't have dogs.[5] Of course, fetch is an excellent option, which I explain how to teach on page 85, chapter 4. A lot of people also like running with their dogs. Always start off slowly; don't try to accomplish a 5K right off the bat. Instead, gradually add distance and increase speed to make sure your dog can handle it. Bring along extra water to help your dog stay hydrated, and, if it's particularly hot or cold out, make accommodations to protect him from the elements. If your dog can tolerate longer distances and it seems you're holding him back from running faster, you can also ride your bike and have him run alongside you. (Discretion is certainly advised here. You'll need to pay attention to your dog, the road, traffic, and any potential distractions. Ideally, practice this in very low-traffic areas such as dead end streets, and hold the leash but never tie it to your bike.) Again, double-check with your vet when you can start running with your dog—some experts advise that you wait until the dog is full-grown. Of course, if running isn't your thing, there are plenty of other activities, many of which I explain in this chapter.

ASK *Zak*

Swim Lessons

"We have a pool in our backyard, and I'm afraid my dog is going to fall in. Will he know how to swim, or do I have to teach him?"

Most dogs instinctively know how to swim; however, this is one area where breed stereotypes (which normally drive me crazy!) actually ring true for the most part. Some dogs instantly love water and jump right in; others can swim but need a little coaching and possibly encouragement. Some breeds should probably avoid the water altogether—for instance, dogs with heavy chests compared to their hind legs, such as Bulldogs, can sink right to the bottom. Brachycephalic breeds—those with pushed-in faces, such as Pugs, Bulldogs, Cavalier King Charles Spaniels, and Boston Terriers—also usually have trouble swimming. Keep in mind that while some small breeds can swim, they'll tire pretty quickly. Same goes for puppies.

Regardless of the type of dog you have and whether or not he's a natural Michael Phelps, it's important to remember that *any* dog can drown in a pool. That's why it's crucial to take the safety precautions that I outlined on page 48, chapter 2, such as installing a pool fence or a motion detector system.

Don't get me wrong—swimming is an excellent, low-impact way to exercise your dog, and I encourage it for most dogs. Here's what to do to ensure safe, happy swimming:

- Consider getting a life vest for your dog for extra protection, at least until you're comfortable that your dog knows how to swim and get out of the pool. Also, if your dog can't swim, a vest can allow him to enjoy pool time with his family.

- Never just toss your dog into the pool to see what happens. That'll likely terrify him and create a negative association with the pool (let alone the fact that it can be dangerous). Your goal should be making the experience as positive as possible. Get into the pool yourself and let your pet run around the perimeter. Entice him closer to the pool by offering treats or toys.

- If at any point you think your dog is overly anxious, take a break. However, if you think he's doing fine, then let him stand briefly on the first step in the pool and see how he does. If he jumps out, that's okay. Try again in a few minutes. If he does great, then reward him and gradually increase the time he spends in the pool. For instance, let him swim a few laps, but always stand right next to him to offer support the second he needs it. You want him to always feel safe.

- At first, you'll have to help your dog get out of the pool by either guiding him to the steps or lifting him out if need be. However, it's important to make sure he learns to do it on his own. So after your dog is comfortable swimming and coming to you while in the water, you should be able to guide him to the pool steps by calling to him just like you do on land. Repeat this often to really make sure he understands where the steps are located.

- Once your dog is done swimming for the day, rinse him off with regular water to wash out any chlorine left on his coat.

Hiking

"Hiking is a big part of my lifestyle. Is it okay to take my dog with me on hikes?"

Absolutely. Hiking is one of the best forms of exercise your dog can do— it stimulates him physically, of course, but with the myriad of sights, smells, and sounds, he'll be mentally engaged as well. That's why most dogs love this activity. However, make sure you take the following safety precautions:

- Bring plenty of water for your dog and a small bowl. Don't let your dog drink from any puddles, lakes, ponds, or other bodies of water—they could contain parasites and other contaminants. Also, if you're hiking long enough that you need to bring snacks for yourself, bring along some food or treats for your dog as well. You may even want to feed him half his daily meal beforehand and then give him the rest halfway through the hike.

- Let your dog off leash only if you are very certain he'll come when called regardless of any distractions (trust me, there will be plenty of those!). Also, double-check that the area you're hiking in permits dogs to wander off leash. Of course, keeping your dog *on* leash can help you navigate him away from any dangers such as poison ivy, broken glass, or other animals you might encounter.

- Sure you're in nature, but you still need to always pick up after your dog. Your fellow hikers will appreciate it! Bring poop bags.

- As always, make sure your dog is up to date with his vaccinations, microchipped, and wearing identification tags.

- Bring along a first aid kit in case your dog gets any bites, scrapes, or other injuries during the hike. (You should have one for yourself, anyway!)

- After your hike, check your dog for fleas and ticks, as well as any critters, burrs, or other "extras" he might have brought back from his adventure.

Dog Parks

"There's a dog park near my house that I was thinking of going to this weekend. Is it worth my time?"

Dog parks are a big wild card. While I'm happy they're available to dogs who do well in this setting, the cons to going to one can outweigh the pros for many dogs. The problem is that you often get a lot of dogs with too much energy in one place. Add to that the fact that many dogs are not immediately accepting of new dogs, and before you know it you've got scuffles breaking out left and right. Also, too many people rely on dog parks for exercising and socializing their dogs. This is where most people go wrong. Your dog's primary exercise should be done with *you*, not with other dogs that he doesn't know.

However, if you want to give the dog park experience a shot, first make sure that your dog is good with other dogs by introducing him to several other dogs in non–dog park situations. If this goes well, consider going to the dog park in off-peak hours. I really don't like to see groups of more than three or four dogs playing at a time unless the dogs regularly play together and always get along. Also, I strongly advise exercising your dog *before* going to the dog park so he'll be a little more subdued and relaxed. In my experience, lack of exercise is the most significant contributor to most fights between dogs. Monitor your dog closely, and if you notice him or other dogs getting too rambunctious, break up the play session.

Service Dogs

"Recently in a restaurant I saw a woman with a dog wearing a service vest. What is that, and is it something I should get for my dog so he can come into restaurants with me, too?"

Definitely not, unless you actually need a service dog. According to the Americans with Disabilities Act (ADA), service animals are dogs trained to perform tasks for people with disabilities, such as "guiding people who are blind, alerting people who are deaf, pulling a wheelchair, alerting and protecting a person who is having a seizure, reminding a person with mental illness to take prescribed medications, calming a person with post traumatic stress disorder (PTSD) during an anxiety attack, or performing other duties."[6] The organization considers these dogs working animals, not pets. A person with one of these dogs can enter places the general public can go, even places where dogs are not normally allowed, such as restaurants, movie theaters, and hospitals.

The problem is, it's very difficult to regulate which dogs are true service dogs and which ones aren't. The ADA stipulates that staff at, say, a restaurant, store, or doctor's office can only ask if the dog is a service animal required because of a disability and, if so, the nature of the animal's particular task or work. Many companies have sadly capitalized on such loose regulations—they'll send a certification and "service" vest over the Internet to just about anybody, usually for a considerable fee.

You may be wondering, "What's the harm in faking it so that my dog can accompany me anywhere?" Unfortunately, it really hurts those who *do* need such dogs. Legitimate service dogs are highly and specifically trained and have a certain temperament that makes them ideal for the job; however, many fake service dogs are not well trained and may behave badly. They might start barking in a restaurant or jumping on people, giving service dogs in general a bad rap. "Every time illegitimate service dogs behave badly, the public is more likely to discriminate against legitimate service dogs," says Paul Mundell, CEO of Canine Companions for Independence. "When a person with a disability relies on a highly trained assistance dog, being denied the right to access public places with their dog will ultimately limit that person's ability to lead an independent life."

Bottom line: If you truly qualify for a service dog, by all means look into getting one. Otherwise, don't take advantage of a service that's meant for people who really require it.

Extracurricular Activities

"My dog is a bundle of energy, and I'd love to do some activities with him outside of basic training. Any suggestions?"

Basic training and tricks can certainly satisfy a lot of dogs, but then there are those with so much energy that they constantly seem to be saying, "I'm not tired yet. Let's do *more*!" Luckily, today there are many recreational options for dogs that can fulfill any need, ranging from herding and tracking to dog surfing and sled dog racing. For instance, I began my dog training career by competing and performing in Frisbee competitions, a really fun dog sport that requires a lot of creativity and originality. My high-energy dogs loved every minute of it.

There are many opportunities out there, and you can find the right one for your dog no matter what his energy level is (yes, even if he's a couch potato!). Do a little research online or ask your veterinarian, local dog clubs, shelters, or other friends with dogs for options. There are no single governing bodies for most dog sports; search for dedicated organizations and clubs in your area to learn more about what each activity has to offer. And be wary: when choosing one, unfortunately you may encounter those who subscribe to outdated training styles. If these groups ever pressure you to use pain or discomfort to train your dog, keep searching. The advice in this book will get you *much* further when participating in the dog sports out there. Trust me, I've competed at the highest levels of dog Frisbee and done lots of exhibition agility, flyball, and other activities with my dogs over the years. Fun is key with dog sports!

The following is a quick overview of some of the more popular activities you may want to consider. Check them out—you'll be amazed by some of the things dogs can do!

AGILITY

In this sport, people direct their dogs through an obstacle course that can include maneuvers such as jumping hurdles, climbing up ramps, going through tunnels, and weaving in and out of poles. Teams are scored based on time and accuracy.

FLYBALL

Teams of four dogs compete against each other in this relay race. The dogs jump hurdles over a fifty-one-foot course, retrieve a ball from a spring-loaded box that they hit, and then return over the jumps.

▶ FLYING DISC COMPETITION

This one is near and dear to my heart! In this activity, commonly referred to as dog Frisbee, a person throws a flying disc at various distances and/ or in a choreographed sequence, ending up with the disc being caught by their dog. It can involve a lot of tricks, too—I loved to incorporate "back stall" and even "play dead" in some of the competitions I did with Venus. If you are active and creative and have a high-energy dog, you may want to get involved.

FREESTYLE

So you think you can dance? Or you think maybe your dog can? Consider this type of competition, in which a person and their dog perform choreographed routines set to music.

DOCK DIVING

This relatively new sport, also known as dock jumping, is becoming increasingly popular. Basically, dogs jump off a dock into water and compete for distance and height. Of course, your dog will have to be a very proficient swimmer to participate in this event.

THERAPY DOGS

Whether or not your dog is the active type, if he's well behaved and friendly to strangers, he may be perfect for what's known as animal-assisted therapy (not to be confused with service dogs). Dogs are trained to offer affection and comfort to people in hospitals, nursing homes, areas that have been affected by a disaster, and schools, or to people with learning disabilities, for example. Research has shown that interacting with an animal can not only lift one's spirits and help reduce anxiety but also lower blood pressure, improve cardiovascular health, and have positive effects on a person's mental and physical well-being in countless other ways.[7]

CONCLUSION

Dogs certainly can enrich our lives and make us better people. They are always there to comfort us, protect us, and do virtually anything we ask of them, and they teach us much more than we could ever teach them. *This* is the great treasure of the Dog Training Revolution. In exchange for these gifts, all dogs ask for in return is that you provide for their basic needs, keep them safe, and give them a little understanding and lots of love. A game of fetch or tug-of-war is usually a hit, too!

I am honored that you took the time to read this book. The good news is that while I've explained how to teach your pet everything from the basic skills and housetraining to really cool tricks, all of my advice will help strengthen your bond with your dog and bring you both to a place of mutual understanding. That close relationship, in turn, will allow you to earn your dog's respect, rather than demanding it, and you will be able to set your expectations much higher. This is the most powerful way to teach a dog, because the real magic happens when you transcend a "step-by-step" approach and connect with each other in a way that's organic.

You now know not only how to teach your dog but also how to care for her in every sense of the word from the first moment she enters your life. Before I met Venus, I never imagined I could have such a rich, meaningful relationship with a dog built on a deep level of communication, trust, love, and understanding. My hope is that after reading this book, you will have a relationship like that with your dog, too.

Welcome to the Dog Training Revolution!

ENDNOTES

INTRODUCTION

1. "Position Statement on the Use of Dominance Theory in Behavior Modification of Animals," American Veterinary Society of Animal Behavior, 2008, accessed November 28, 2014. http://avsabonline.org/uploads/position_statements/dominance_statement.pdf; "Dominance and Dog Training," Association of Professional Dog Trainers, 2009, accessed December 2, 2014, https://apdt.com/about/position-statements/dominance/.

CHAPTER ONE. DECISIONS, DECISIONS

1. "Pet Statistics," American Society for the Prevention of Cruelty to Animals, accessed December 3, 2014, https://www.aspca.org/about-us/faq/pet-statistics.
2. "Dog Breedopedia," petMD, accessed December 3, 2014, http://www.petmd.com/dog/breeds.
3. Cornelia Kraus et al., "The Size–Life Span Trade-Off Decomposed: Why Large Dogs Die Young," *American Naturalist* 181, no. 4 (2013): 492–505.
4. Thomas P. Bellumori et al., "Prevalence of Inherited Disorders Among Mixed-Breed and Purebred Dogs: 27,254 Cases (1995–2010)," *Journal of the American Veterinary Medical Association* 242, no. 11 (2013): 1549–1555.

5. Stanley Coren, "A Designer Dog Maker Regrets His Creation," *Psychology Today*, April 1, 2014, https://www.psychologytoday.com/blog/canine-corner/201404/designer-dog-maker-regrets-his-creation.

6. "Adopting from an Animal Shelter or Rescue Group," Humane Society of the United States, March 19, 2013, http://www.humanesociety.org/issues/adopt/tips/adopting_from_shelter_rescue.html.

7. AKC Rescue Network, American Kennel Club, http://www.akc.org/dog-breeds/rescue-network/.

8. "How to Find a Responsible Dog Breeder," Humane Society of the United States, last updated 2012, http://www.humanesociety.org/assets/pdfs/pets/puppy_mills/find_responsible_dog_breeder.pdf.

9. Franklin D. McMillan et al., "Differences in Behavioral Characteristics Between Dogs Obtained as Puppies from Pet Stores and Those Obtained from Noncommercial Breeders," *Journal of the American Veterinary Medical Association* 242, no. 10 (2013): 1359–1363.

10. "Pet Allergies," Asthma and Allergy Foundation of America, last updated 2005, https://www.aafa.org/display.cfm?id=9&sub=18&cont=236.

11. Charlotte E. Nicholas et al., "Dog Allergen Levels in Homes with Hypoallergenic Compared with Nonhypoallergenic Dogs," *American Journal of Rhinology & Allergy* 25, no. 4 (2011): 252–256.

12. Jaclyn E. Barnes et al., "Ownership of High-Risk ('Vicious') Dogs as a Marker for Deviant Behaviors: Implications for Risk Assessment," *Journal of Interpersonal Violence* 21, no. 12 (2006): 1616–1634.

13. Gary J. Patronek et al., "Co-occurrence of Potentially Preventable Factors in 256 Dog Bite–Related Fatalities in the United States (2000–2009)," *Journal of the American Veterinary Medical Association* 243, no. 12 (2013): 1726–1736.

14. "Breed-Specific Policies: No Basis in Science," Humane Society of the United States, March, 24, 2015, http://www.humanesociety.org/issues/breed-specific-legislation/fact_sheets/breed-specific-legislation-no-basis-in-science.html.

15. "Types of Dogs Prohibited in Great Britain," Department for Environmental Food and Rural Affairs, 2003, accessed December 10, 2014, http://web.archive.org/web/20070309200431/http://www.defra.gov.uk/animalh/welfare/domestic/ddogsleaflet.pdf.

16. Kathryn M. Wrubel et al., "Interdog Household Aggression: 38 Cases (2006–2007)," *Journal of the American Veterinary Medical Association* 238, no. 6 (2011): 731–740.

CHAPTER TWO. BEFORE YOUR DOG COMES HOME

1. "Questions and Answers Regarding Pet Jerky Treats," U.S. Food and Drug Administration, last updated February 19, 2015, http://www.fda.gov /AnimalVeterinary/SafetyHealth/ProductSafetyInformation/ucm295445 .htm.

2. "Foods That Are Hazardous to Dogs," American Society for the Prevention of Cruelty to Animals, accessed December 20, 2014, https://www.aspca.org/pet-care/virtual-pet-behaviorist/dog-behavior /foods-are-hazardous-dogs.

3. "Toxic and Nontoxic Plants," American Society for the Prevention of Cruelty to Animals, accessed December 20, 2014, https://www.aspca .org/pet-care/animal-poison-control/toxic-and-non-toxic-plants.

4. Rebecca F. Wisch, "Table of State Laws Concerning Minimum Age for Sale of Puppies," Michigan State University Animal Legal & Historical Center, 2015, www.animallaw.info/topic/table-state-laws-concerning-minimum-age-sale-puppies.

5. "Ear Cropping and Tail Docking of Dogs," American Veterinary Medical Association, accessed December 22, 2014, https://www.avma.org /KB/Policies/Pages/Ear-Cropping-and-Tail-Docking-of-Dogs.aspx.

6. G. J. Noonan et al., "Behavioral Observations of Puppies Undergoing Tail Docking," *Applied Animal Behaviour Science* 49, no. 4 (1996): 335–342; Jamie L. LaPrairie and Anne Z. Murphy, "Long-Term Impact of Neonatal Injury in Male and Female Rats: Sex Differences, Mechanisms and Clinical Implications," *Frontiers in Neuroendocrinology* 31, no. 2 (2010): 193–202; David Vega-Avelaira et al., "The Emergence of Adolescent Onset Pain Hypersensitivity Following Neonatal Nerve Injury," *Molecular Pain* 8 (2012): 30.

CHAPTER THREE. WELCOME TO THE FAMILY

1. "Dog Bite Prevention," American Veterinary Medical Association, accessed January 15, 2015, https://www.avma.org/public/Pages/Dog-Bite-Prevention.aspx.

2. "Pets by the Numbers," Humane Society of the United States, January 30, 2014, http://www.humanesociety.org/issues/pet_overpopulation/facts/pet_ownership_statistics.html.

3. "Common Sense Measures to Protect Your Dog, Yourself, and Others in Canine Social Settings," American Veterinary Medical Association, https://www.avma.org/public/PetCare/Pages/Protect-Your-Dogs-Yourself-and-Others.aspx.

4. Deborah Miller et al., "Factors Associated with the Decision to Surrender a Pet to an Animal Shelter," *Journal of the American Veterinary Medical Association* 209, no. 4 (1996): 738–742.

5. Mayo Clinic, "Dog Tired? It Could Be Your Pooch," *Science Daily,* February 15, 2002, http://www.sciencedaily.com/releases/2002/02/020215070932.htm.

6. "AVSAB Position Statement on Puppy Socialization," American Veterinary Society of Animal Behavior, 2008, accessed January 15, 2015, http://avsabonline.org/uploads/position_statements/puppy_socialization.pdf.

7. Meredith E. Stepita et al., "Frequency of CPV Infection in Vaccinated Puppies That Attended Puppy Socialization Classes," *Journal of the American Animal Hospital Association* 49, no. 2 (2013): 95–100.

CHAPTER FOUR. DOG TRAINING REVOLUTION

1. "What Are Some of the Common Myths About Dog Training?" Association of Professional Dog Trainers, accessed January 20, 2015, https://apdt.com/pet-owners/choosing-a-trainer/myths/.

2. L. David Mech, "Alpha Status, Dominance, and Division of Labor in Wolf Packs," *Canadian Journal of Zoology* 77 (1999): 1196–1203. http://www.wolf.org/wp-content/uploads/2013/09/267alphastatus_english.pdf.

3. Meghan E. Herron et al., "Survey of the Use and Outcome of Confrontational and Non-confrontational Training Methods in Client-Owned Dogs Showing Undesired Behaviors," *Applied Animal Behaviour Science* 117, no. 1–2 (2009): 47–54.

4. "The Meaning and Origin of the Expression: You Can't Teach an Old Dog New Tricks," Phrase Finder, accessed January 23, 2015, http://www.phrases.org.uk/meanings/you-cant-teach-an-old-dog-new-tricks.html.

5. Claudia Kawczynska, "Neuroscientist Gregory Berns Reveals What Dogs Are Thinking," *The Bark*, accessed January 27, 2015, http://the-bark.com/content/neuroscientist-gregory-berns-reveals-what-dogs-are-thinking.

6. John W. Wiley and Hilary Hinzmann, *Chaser: Unlocking the Genius of the Dog Who Knows a Thousand Words* (New York: Mariner, 2014).

7. David S. Tuber et al., "Behavioral and Glucocorticoid Responses of Adult Domestic Dogs (*Canis familiaris*) to Companionship and Social Separation," *Journal of Comparative Psychology* 110, no. 1 (1996): 103–108.

8. Andrea Beetz et al., "Psychosocial and Psychophysiological Effects of Human-Animal Interactions: The Possible Role of Oxytocin," *Frontiers in Psychology* 3 (2012): 234; Miho Nagasawa et al., "Oxytocin-Gaze Positive Loop and the Coevolution of Human-Dog Bonds," *Science*, 348, no. 6232 (2015): 333–336.

9. Lisa Horn et al., "The Importance of the Secure Base Effect for Domestic Dogs—Evidence from a Manipulative Problem-Solving Task," *PLoS ONE* 8, no. 5 (2013).

10. Brian Hare, "Dr. Brian Hare: Discovering How Dogs Think," www.purina.com, August 13, 2014, https://www.purina.com/better-with-pets/summit/all-talks/archived-talks/discovering-how-dogs-think.

11. Alexandra Horowitz, *Inside of a Dog: What Dogs See, Smell, and Know* (New York: Scribner, 2009).

12. Brian Hare and Vanessa Woods, *The Genius of Dogs: How Dogs Are Smarter Than You Think* (New York: Dutton, 2013).

13. Ibid.

CHAPTER FIVE. HOUSETRAINING 101

1. "Crate Training," Humane Society of the United States, October 31, 2014, http://www.humanesociety.org/animals/dogs/tips/crate_training.html.

CHAPTER SEVEN. HOW TO TROUBLESHOOT THE MOST COMMON BEHAVIOR PROBLEMS

1. *Dogs: Their Secret Lives*, "Revisited: Results from Emily Blackwell's Survey," video, 2:01. http://dogs.channel4.com/revisited/.

2. American College of Veterinary Behaviorists, *Decoding Your Dog: Explaining Common Dog Behaviors and How to Prevent or Change Unwanted Ones* (New York: Mariner Books, 2015).

3. Rachel A. Casey, "Human Directed Aggression in Domestic Dogs (*Canis familiaris*): Occurrence in Different Contexts and Risk Factors," *Applied Animal Behaviour Science* 152 (2014): 52–63; Dorit Feddersen-Petersen, "Biology of Aggression in Dogs," *Dtsch Tierarztl Wochenschr* 108, no. 3 (2001): 94–101.

4. American College of Veterinary Behaviorists, *Decoding Your Dog.*

CHAPTER EIGHT. IN SICKNESS AND IN HEALTH

1. "Seven Things You Can Do to Keep Your Pet Healthy," American Veterinary Medical Association, accessed March 3, 2015, https://www.avma.org/public/PetCare/Pages/pet-health.aspx.

2. "Raw or Undercooked Animal-Source Protein in Cat and Dog Diets," American Veterinary Medical Association, accessed March 10, 2015, http://www.avma.org/KB/Policies/Pages/Raw-or-Undercooked-Animal-Source-Protein-in-Cat-and-Dog-Diets.aspx; "Pet Food and Treats—Tips for Keeping People and Pets Healthy and Safe from *Salmonella*," Centers for Disease Control and Prevention, last updated September 3, 2013, http://www.cdc.gov/features/salmonelladrypetfood/.

3. Lisa M. Freeman et al., "Current Knowledge About the Risk and Benefits of Raw Meat-Based Diets for Dogs and Cats," *Journal of the American Veterinary Medical Association* 243, no. 11 (2013): 1549–1558.

4. Bob Considine, "Dog's Death Is a Warning About Groomers, Experts Say," www.today.com, August 1, 2008, http://www.today.com/id/25966380/ns/today-today_pets/t/dogs-death-warning-about-groomers-expert-says/.

5. "Spaying and Neutering," American Veterinary Medical Association, accessed March 25, 2015, https://www.avma.org/public/PetCare/Pages/spay-neuter.aspx.

6. Karen Halligan, *Doc Halligan's What Every Pet Owner Should Know* (New York: Collins, 2007).

7. "Heartworm Basics," American Heartworm Society, accessed April 3, 2015, https://www.heartwormsociety.org/newsroom/background-information.

8. "Pets in Vehicles," American Veterinary Medical Association, accessed April 10, 2015, https://www.avma.org/public/PetCare/Pages/pets-in-vehicles.aspx.

9. "Winter Safety and Comfort for Dogs," Association of Professional Dog Trainers, accessed April 20, 2015, https://apdt.com/pet-owners/safety/winter/.

CHAPTER NINE. TIME FOR FUN

1. "Traveling: Should Your Pet Stay or Go?" Humane Society of the United States, June 19, 2013, http://www.humanesociety.org/animals/resources/tips/travelling_with_pets.html.

2. "Air Travel Consumer Reports," United States Department of Transportation, last updated May 11, 2015, accessed May 27, 2015, http://www.dot.gov/airconsumer/air-travel-consumer-reports.

3. "Animal Welfare Act and Animal Welfare Regulations," United States Department of Agriculture, November 2013, http://www.aphis.usda.gov/animal_welfare/downloads/Animal%20Care%20Blue%20Book%20-%202013%20-%20FINAL.pdf; "Plane Talk: Traveling with Animals," United States Department of Transportation, last updated November 2014, http://www.dot.gov/airconsumer/plane-talk-traveling-animals.

4. "Travel with a Pet," United States Department of Agriculture Animal and Plant Health Inspection Service, last updated October 22, 2014, http://www.aphis.usda.gov/wps/portal/aphis/ourfocus/importexport/sa_animals/sa_pet_travel.

5. Hayley Cutt et al., "Understanding Dog Owners' Increased Levels of Physical Activity: Results From RESIDE," *American Journal of Public Health* 98, no. 1 (2008): 66–69.

6. "Service Animals," United States Department of Justice; Civil Rights Division, Disability Rights Section, July 12, 2011, http://www.ada.gov/service_animals_2010.htm.

7. Andrea Beetz et al., "Psychosocial and Psychophysiological Effects of Human-Animal Interactions: The Possible Role of Oxytocin," *Frontiers in Psychology* 3 (2012): 234.

© Rachel Goyette

ZAK GEORGE

Zak George is a trainer who has worked with thousands of dogs since he started his career in 2004. His YouTube channel, *Zak George's Dog Training Revolution*, is the number one destination for video dog training content in the world, receiving more than ten million views annually.

Zak has also starred in two of his own dog training shows, Animal Planet's *Superfetch* and the BBC's *Who Let the Dogs Out?* He has appeared as an expert on various other Animal Planet shows such as *Dogs 101*, while his expertise has landed him on many national television shows such as *Late Night with David Letterman, Late Night with Jimmy Fallon, The Early Show* on CBS, *Fox and Friends*, and *Rachael Ray*.

Zak's goal is to raise the standards in the dog training industry as he advocates for the latest in scientific understanding of dog behavior while balancing this approach with twenty-first-century ethics. He also heavily emphasizes the importance of prioritizing the relationship with our dogs in order to achieve incredible results.

Zak lives in New Orleans with his girlfriend, Bree; their dogs, Venus, Supernova, Alpha Centauri, and Indy; and their cat, Angela.

© Larry Port

DINA ROTH PORT

Dina Roth Port is an award-winning journalist and author of *Previvors: Facing the Breast Cancer Gene and Making Life-Changing Decisions* (Penguin, 2010).

She launched her freelance writing career in 2002, and since then her articles have appeared in many print and online publications such as *Glamour, Self, Prevention, Fitness, Cosmopolitan, Parenting, iVillage.com, Parents.com, The Huffington Post, FitPregnancy.com, Scholastic.com,* and *Martha Stewart Weddings.* A graduate of Northwestern University's Medill School of Journalism, Dina has also worked as an editor at *Glamour* and *Parenting* magazines.

Dina lives in Boca Raton, Florida, with her husband, Larry, and their two children. Of course, her family wouldn't be complete without their beloved pets: Baxter, Brody, and Kitty Cupcake.

INDEX

sleeping and, 110
swimming, 49, 204–5
training after, 84, 116
during workweek, 47, 48
See also Walks
Eye contact, 87
Eyes
care of, 174
communication cues
with, 90
personality and, 29

F

Family
introducing new dog to,
53–57
preparing, for new dog,
44–45
readiness of, for pets, 10, 11
See also Children
Fear, 69–70, 186–87
Female dogs
male vs., 24–25
spaying, 25, 176–77
Fences
backyard, 39
pool, 48–49
Fetch, playing, 85, 96–97
Fleas, 179–80
Flowers, 38–39
Flyball, 209
Flying disc competitions, 210
Food
allergies, 171–72
begging for, 163–64
bowl for, 33
choosing, 170–71

dangerous, 38, 182–83
guarding, 156–57
meal frequency, 171
for new dog, 33
quantity of, 171
raw diets, 172
stealing, 161–63
switching, 33, 66
See also Treats
Freestyle competitions, 210

G

Garlic, 38
Gates, 33
Gender, 24–25
German Shepherd, 16, 23
Giardia, 181
Golden Retriever, 23
Grapes, 38
Great Dane, 16, 42
Greetings, 137–39, 150
Greyhound, 34
Grooming, 34–35, 173–76
Guests, jumping on,
137–39, 150

H

Hand signals, 87–88
Harnesses, 34
Havanese, 17
Head collars, 137
Health insurance, 39–40, 46
Heartworm, 180–81
Hiking, 206
Hot weather, 183–84
House, leaving, 112–13
Houseplants, 38–39, 183

supplies for, 36, 121

time for, 8, 142

traditional, 3, 71–74, 83, 140

"yes" and "no" in, 76, 120–21

See also individual training issues

Travel

accommodations during, 202–3

by airplane, 200–202

by car, 198–200

crates for, 32

as lifestyle issue, 24

Treats, 36, 77–78, 143.

See also Rewards

Tulips, 39

U

"Up," 81, 125, 126–27

Urination. *See* Housetraining

V

Vaccinations, 40–41, 67–68, 178–79

Veterinarians

choosing, 45–47

education of, 46

fear of, 186–87

first visit to, 66–67

importance of relationship with, 45, 169–70

symptoms requiring visit to, 177–78

See also Medical issues

W

Walks

accidents after, 112

housetraining and, 102

on leash, 104–5, 135–37, 147–48

See also Dog walkers; Exercise

"Watch me," 122–23, 124–25

Water bowl, 33

Weather

cold, 184–85

hot, 183–84

Welsh Corgi, 16

West Highland Terrier, 17

Workweek, care during, 47–48

Worms, 41, 180–81

X

Xylitol, 38

Y

Yeast dough, 38

"Yes," 76, 120–21

Yorkie, 15, 34

Published in the United States by Ten Speed Press,
an imprint of the Crown Publishing Group, a division of
Penguin Random House LLC, New York.

www.crownpublishing.com

www.tenspeed.com

Ten Speed Press and the Ten Speed Press colophon
are registered trademarks
of Penguin Random House LLC.

Library of Congress Cataloging-in-Publication Data
Names: George, Zak, author. | Port, Dina Roth, author.
Title: Zak George's dog training revolution : a complete guide to raising the
perfect pet with love / Zak George, with Dina Roth Port.
Other titles: Dog training revolution
Description: First edition. | New York : Ten Speed Press, 2016.
Includes bibliographical references and index.
Identifiers: LCCN 2015048364 (print) | LCCN 2016011071 (ebook)
ISBN 9781607748915 (pbk. : alk. paper) | ISBN 9781607748922 (ebook)
Subjects: LCSH: Dogs--Training. | Dogs.
Classification: LCC SF431 .G43 2016 (print) | LCC SF431 (ebook) |
DDC 636.7/0835--dc23
LC record available at http://lccn.loc.gov/2015048364

Trade Paperback ISBN: 978-1-60774-891-5
eBook ISBN: 978-1-60774-892-2

Printed in the United States of America

Design by Kara Plikaitis
Front cover photograph copyright © Daymon Gardner

14 16 18 20 19 17 15

First Edition